# PUTTING
# PHILOSOPHY
## IN ITS PLACE

## A PREFACE TO THE LIFE OF PHILOSOPHY

**Kendall Hunt**
p u b l i s h i n g   c o m p a n y

**LARRY D. HARWOOD**
*Viterbo University*

Cover image courtesy of Dorothy J. Almen-Harwood

# Kendall Hunt
publishing company

www.kendallhunt.com
*Send all inquiries to*:
4050 Westmark Drive
Dubuque, IA 52004-1840

Copyright © 2014 by Kendall Hunt Publishing Company

ISBN 978-1-4652-3989-1

Printed in the United States of America
10 9 8 7 6 5 4 3 2 1

For Theodore Kristian

The history of philosophy, like history in general, aims at replacing a naïve relation with the past with one that is more thoughtful. It implies an intention to strangle legends.

Rémi Brague

# Contents

# Preface

This book is written for the students of philosophy who resist philosophy as an unworthy subject of study. To that end, the book is thus not meant to berate beginners or even antagonists for a negative impression of philosophy. The intent of the words and explanations and stories on these few pages is to ask the reticent student to consider philosophy as a worthy companion for life. To have some success with a rather Herculean task in such a brief book, I willingly concede some criticisms of philosophy as not only understandable but sometimes justified, and so the hesitant student will hear his own critical voice at times in this text. Such an admission, however, need not detract from the affirmation in these pages of the Socratic purposes of philosophy—for life and for a certain kind of life. By conceding imperfections in practicing philosophy in the history of philosophy, I simply affirm that there are different conceptions of philosophy practiced throughout the world and in the history of philosophy. In these pages, therefore, philosophy is critiqued as it is at the same time applauded in its Socratic form.

To the philosopher who undertakes to read this book, it will be apparent that my topic could be pursued from various perspectives. However, because the book is written for students, I have chosen to highlight philosophy from the perspective of the Socratic tradition. This is simply because it is within that tradition that philosophy possesses great potential for redirecting and changing human lives. When the new and probably leery student of philosophy makes inquiry about how philosophy interfaces with life, starting with that tradition is a most fitting place from which to begin philosophy.

# Acknowledgments

This book is written out of my experience as a teacher of philosophy at Viterbo University. A few among my many students are responsible for a memorable question or story that has found its way into this book. Therefore, to those philosophy students of the past and present at Viterbo University, I am grateful. Their puzzlement over what philosophy is and what to do with philosophy has been my immediate impetus to write this little book.

To my wife Dottie, I owe thanks for always listening to my cache of stories about student reactions to a subject mystifying to many.

With sincere gratitude I thank my Dean at Viterbo University, Dr. Glena Temple, for her unwavering and always helpful support. To my department head, Dr. Bill Reese, I owe hearty thanks for his patience and for infinite kindness extended to a department member whose projects were not always predictable until finished.

To Lindsay Cummings, I extend thanks as a reader of a chapter of the manuscript and for suggesting many helpful corrections. To Judy Ulland, I wish to convey my upmost thanks for having read the entire manuscript meticulously. Her aid and encouragement have been immeasurable to me in this project.

# Chapter 1

# The Problem of Philosophy

## 1.1 The Oddity of Philosophy and Philosophers

Philosophers appear odd because philosophy seems so deliberately odd, with its practitioners engaged with a subject toward which most other people feel little inclination. Of course, philosophy hardly existed before philosophers contemplated questions that in time came to be called philosophical and these thinkers called philosophers. Thus the first question about philosophy concerns the kind of people producing a subject so unattractive to many disinterested others. However peculiar the subject of philosophy is, even more inscrutable would seem the people not only doing but also enjoying philosophy.

To understand philosophers, we might start from observations anyone might make. For philosophers, our common notions about things in the world and the truth about them are debatable and open to question. This is because there is a bit—most philosophers would say a lot—of ambiguity and cause for puzzlement about the world, necessitating a thorough inquiry for the elusive truth of the matter on their many questions. If we conjecture that the questions of philosophers are by design meant to bring the house down, we misunderstand them. They will say that it is not destruction by intention but the belief, very strong among philosophers, that getting to the truth of the matter requires making judgments and sorting out the contenders for the desired goal of truth.

One thus easily sees that philosophers rarely take the world as they find it. This feature almost immediately qualifies them as different from others. That is, they are easily noticed as persistent questioners and proverbial doubters. It is not that they think themselves hoodwinked and undertake a vendetta against the world; rather they see many things in the world as provokingly puzzling. They desire to scrutinize so as to understand, with the tendency to call anything into question, whereas others may simply accept whatever is, as it is. Philosophers seem incurably curious and deliberative to a fault and likely innocent of the realization that such traits perceived in excess may annoy their peers. Such a tendency of the philosopher to question and doubt well-nigh everything can offend others, who may judge the philosopher as vain and judgmental for implying that others simply and mindlessly acquiesce with the majority.

Nevertheless, philosophers are partly as they are because they have doubts about the world—about, for instance, what is real and not mere appearance—and a host of other issues. Philosophers would say that the world we live in begs questions. The German philosopher Schopenhauer (1788–1860) said something nearly like that when he wrote that life is a problem; therefore, philosophy begins by addressing a host of issues or problems that life presents for the living—unless the living are asleep. The philosopher is actively combating the temptation to sleep while he is awake, for he doggedly resists being consciously mistaken about the truth as he looks and reasons and makes judgments to approach his goal. This produces in the philosopher a certain restlessness, a trait probably less common among peers who feel more comfortable with their inherited world.

Individuals drawn to questioning as a habit of mind may encounter something giving them pause to consider old things in new ways—or, for that matter, new things in old ways. This may be something beyond natural curiosity, for an uninterrupted life might easily miss what the nudge of pain or the uncomfortable or the unfamiliar may prod people to conceive or imagine or doubt. We might then say that people for the most part and maybe most of the time are not naturally exercising their curiosity nor habitually prying into the secrets of life and the world because they are rather prone to leave well enough alone for as long as things are well. On the other hand, situations in life may be a precipitating factor shoving some people toward questions scarcely considered previously.

Of course, there is neither an absolute nor an unwavering divide between the inquisitive people and noninquisitive types, such that there are simply few inquisitive among us—the philosophers—and remaining are the noninquisitive. If natural curiosity and life are often sufficient of themselves to spark questions from virtually all people either sooner or later, then we can erase any absolute distinction between the presumed very odd philosophers and the very normal everyone else, for everyone is curious to some degree, at least in the beginning of life.

Moreover, one notices that people manifestly share in a natural and persistent human inquisitiveness in childhood. Scarcely anyone thinks children odd for what we might call their natural youthful curiosity because we expect such a trait in children. However, when an adult dares to become extraordinarily inquisitive again, this individual may incur quizzical looks for questions deemed settled some time ago—or so this adult may be told by other annoyed adults. Such an individual may provoke the ire of the surrounding world, in contrast to the expected and welcomed inquisitiveness of that same person as a child.

Because philosophers are apt to regard the world with a protracted sense of childlike puzzlement, they rarely feel complacent. Philosophers moreover tend to be people who are independently minded and whose interests often set them apart from others. They may consequently exhibit a restlessness that gives them only rare interludes to agree with others. This trait may make them solitary and indifferent toward much of their surroundings. And yet, they are not asleep, only submerged in their thinking so as to appear asleep. To philosophers, it is likely everyone else who is asleep, and yet these awakened people may rarely notice the resting sleepers, who could not possibly miss the restless philosophers. With philosophers seeming aloof from much of the ordinary world, they may be thought of as less than warm people, perhaps even cold, or at least people not living anywhere but in their head.

An example of this perception of philosophers struck me several years ago when I shared an office with another professor of philosophy. In the beginning of a semester, we suddenly realized we had no sign on our door to indicate that students were welcome to stop for scheduling, signatures, and the like. Upon this realization, my colleague hastily pulled out a blank sheet of paper and printed on it the words, "Feel Free to Knock if Door is Closed," and we posted it on the door. A couple of days later while coming to work I noticed that someone, presumably a student, had marked through the word "Feel" and substituted the word "Think." The point of course was that philosophers do not feel; they think. Philosophers were in effect perceived as thinking machines—logical, rational, and cerebral—to the student scribbler. Whatever other traits humans might possess, such as emotions or something close to feelings, did not seem to occupy the domain of philosophers—at least in the mind of the anonymous student who renewed our attention to how students see these odd people called philosophers.

The peculiar subject of philosophy precipitates another and more grave hesitation from students who surmise nervously that they lack a sufficiently able mind for philosophy. This is because philosophy is commonly thought of as devoting time to "deep" or difficult questions: the kind the philosopher is supposed to ruminate about and about which the doubting student may have had prior doubts. Nevertheless, while fear of lacking an intellect sufficient to engage such questions may make some students dread philosophy, probably the strongest aversion arises from the perception that such a subject robs time away from more weighty and practical matters, about which nebulous philosophy has little to contribute. Philosophy is therefore often resented as something of a leisure activity that wastes a lot of time and is rather a noncontributor in the real world. Although plenty of philosophers have been seen as radicals or troublemakers or vain or simply stubborn, this charge is that they are wasteful for focusing energies upon enterprises that are worthless for real work of real worth. The head and feet of philosophers are not planted on the earth, but in the air, rendering them at best harmless amusements for the rest of us, or at worst, squanderers of intellectual plenty.

Although philosophers have been notorious for being oblivious to their surroundings, the tranquility of the life of the philosopher can be an envied spectacle to people otherwise annoyed by perceived aloofness. Plutarch (c. 46–120 AD), the ancient Greek historian, records an amusing incident where Alexander the Great (356–323 BC), who had been tutored by the Greek philosopher Aristotle (384–322 BC) during his youth, visits the philosopher Diogenes of Sinope (412–323 BC).

> Diogenes of Sinope, who then was living in Corinth, thought so little of [Alexander], that instead of coming to compliment him, he never so much as stirred out of the suburb called the Cranium, where Alexander found him lying alone in the sun. When he saw so much company near him, he raised himself a little, and vouchsafed to look upon Alexander, and when he [Alexander] kindly asked him whether he wanted anything, "Yes," said he, "I would have you stand from between me and the sun." Alexander was so struck at this answer, and surprised at the greatness of the man, who had taken so little notice of him, that as he went away he told his followers, who were laughing at the moroseness of the philosopher, that if he were not Alexander, he would choose to be Diogenes.

Plato (427–347 BC) records the story that Thales (c. 624–c. 546 BC), also an ancient philosopher, fell into a well while gazing at the stars, and Plato went on to add that Thales is not unique among philosophers for a lack of finesse with the everyday world. Thus we can conjecture that if philosophers are to be measured by their ability to deal ably with negotiating the ordinary world, most would sputter while others require aid because by largely living in their head, they can be very inept at ordinary living, or even—as Diogenes—indifferent to the point of great oddity to most others. However, part of the resistance toward philosophers is to discount or dismiss them for any use they might be to the world as thinkers for the reason that they appear failures as doers. That is, philosophers are often satirized as if their oddities or fumbling incompetence in practical matters renders them useless for much of anything truly useful. In such a conclusion, little to no room is left for philosophy. To the critic, in a world of practical living there is no space for the philosopher judged incompetent in the only issues that seem to matter to such a critic. In his satirical *Praise of Folly* the Renaissance figure Erasmus (c. 1466–1536) provides such an example of this kind of criticism of philosophers:

> It could be borne if philosophers only approached public affairs as asses do a lyre, but they have no dexterity whatsoever in any common function of life. Invite a wise man to a feast and he will spoil it either by a gloomy silence or asking a lot of bothersome questions. Ask him to a dance and you will see how a camel dances. Take him to a play and by his expression he will dampen the mirth of the people. . . . If something is to be bought, or a contract to be made, or, in short, if anything is to be done without which this daily life is unable to go on, you would call this "genius" not a man but simply deadwood. He can be of no use to himself, his country, or his family because he is completely unskilled in the affairs of daily life and because he is so far removed from the common way of thinking and living; and for this reason he cannot help but be odious to the common folk because of the great diversity between their lives and his.

Erasmus evokes a common sentiment toward philosophers because of the tendency of humans to denigrate matters judged as having little relevance to real lives. People for all time have habitually regarded philosophy as a dubious exercise by such reasoning. However, what Erasmus refers to as "the common way of thinking and living" probably only reflects the suspicion of anything deemed "impractical." Behind the objection, moreover, is the charge that philosophy is void of practical use. Meanwhile, the critic is apt to ignore and thus miss the fact that life may be rather empty until it is questioned.

The indictment of philosophy as an irritant, or "odious," as Erasmus puts it, is sustained by the particularly modern tendency of regarding the purpose of knowledge and knowing as lending tangible, physical support to lives always needful of more such support. Whereas historically this motivation may first be one of simply trying to acquire knowledge enough so as to fend off deadly diseases and disasters of various sorts, it may evolve precipitously into eat, drink, and be merry because there is nothing else to do or even worth doing. What may begin as a justification of knowledge as tangibly aiding material lives suffering from diseases and various other maladies may end by demanding there be no detour from the kind of life that removes inconveniences from life for the sole goal of improved physical life.

Usually at this point, the name of Francis Bacon (1561–1626) comes up. Bacon is one of those harbingers of ages to provide a pivot for turning culture in one direction and significantly away from another. Whether fair to Bacon or not, the negative judgment charges Bacon as one of the thinkers instilling into the nascent modern Western culture the notion that the purpose of knowledge is not knowledge for its own sake but for the sake of something else—improving upon our physical or material condition, such that dreaded diseases and disasters are subdued so that human knowledge is seen as improving the human physical condition. His statement most often associated with this idea is that "Knowledge is power."

Of course, one purpose in our exploration of philosophy is to consider why the critic is convinced of the oddity of the philosopher from the critic's perspective. One reason is that our culture, having largely absorbed much of the idea about the material purposes of knowledge, presumes that one can live happily with the material betterments that we have possessed in gargantuan quantity since the time of Bacon and that these are deemed sufficient for the kind of life we wish to lead. However, the irritating philosopher might object that the human can be impoverished by a life that may be lived with material plenty and little else besides the desired physical ends of life.

The philosopher's want or insistence for some serious thinking about significant matters, however, can appear a killjoy as the philosopher seems to live in a past that for the critic has happily been passed over for a present in which the ideas the philosopher wants to discuss, and the way he wants to discuss them, tempt no one, or paltry few. Philosophy talk or considerations are simply regarded as void of any relevance to the present life. It suspiciously looks as if the philosopher is up to nothing that anybody wants.

The oddity of philosophy in the world extends deeper still to the parents of students who probably pause upon learning they have a son or daughter contemplating a major in philosophy. Moreover, like some hesitant parents of budding philosophers, some philosophers—the people we are trying to understand—have had occasional but grave doubts over the profession they practice. For philosophers can manifest worries—not about their general incompetence in practical affairs—but troubling doubts about the actual value of their work as philosophers. Indeed, philosophy is one of those professions where practitioners may experience halting doubt—though fortunately usually temporary—about the worthiness of their profession for the time and energy of adults. The medical doctor or engineer or cosmetologist or farmer or software programmer is probably much less likely to confront such doubt about his work as lacking a sufficient reason in its purpose. Therefore, with philosophers we confront the oddity that some exhibit the same worry about the worthiness of their subject that many critics share. So whereas we suggested in the beginning of this chapter that understanding the philosopher might aid in understanding philosophy, now we glimpse the reality that some philosophers are sometimes doubtful of doing philosophy.

Part of the problem with philosophy for all groups—students, parents of students, some philosophers, and certainly many onlookers finding philosophers odious—is that philosophy has an intangible product; this feature of philosophy of course is apt to make many people think it really does nothing. This perception, moreover, particularly illustrates our modern tendency to regard the tangible and physical components of our lives as more fundamental or maybe even exhausting the sum total of what we believe about life or about ourselves. That is, the material and technological world is so much a part of our lives today that we are prone to regard a real discussion of ideas, as in philosophy, as a vacuous enterprise with no pertinence to a real world that has left behind the antiquated world of ideas for the increasingly controllable and comfortable present. This is perhaps why some disturbance in life may spur one toward philosophy.

Doubt about the worthiness of philosophy has nevertheless plagued some of the most notable and gifted philosophers of history. In his *Autobiography*, Bertrand Russell (1872–1970), a philosophical giant of the twentieth century, wrote about that time in his life when he was trying to solve the problem of logical paradoxes and would stare for days, eight-hour days—the same as a real work day—at a blank sheet of paper. With such nonproductivity staring back at him, he began to surmise "that my time was spent in considering matters that seemed unworthy of serious attention." Russell went on to write that he turned away from logic before and during World War I because it made no sense to give oneself to issues whose importance depended on having human beings around to think about them. Practical and dire matters usurped his passion for philosophy—for a while.

For Russell, the worthiness of subject matter for human reflection presumes the continuation of human existence itself. His point is easily understood but can also be applied to include the painter, the cosmetologist, the software programmer, and virtually all others who might also reevaluate themselves and their work in such a dire situation. Philosophy might not fare worse than anything else and indeed probably find more place in the confrontation with such a predicament. That is, in times of dire trouble, philosophy could show its mettle by producing a state of mind of extraordinary clarity and fortitude in the face of onerous circumstances. The situation might provoke focus on some things that matter more than the details that absorb most of us during the times when life is good. This is why we refer to someone in distress who nonetheless appears composed as being "philosophical about it." The Roman philosopher Boethius (c. 480–525/6 AD), who lived at the time when the old Roman Empire had crumbled before the invading Germanic tribes, provides a classic example of the "saving" power of philosophy. While awaiting execution for the charge of treason under Theodoric (c. 454–526), the king of the tribe of the Ostrogoths, Boethius wrote his famous work *Consolation of Philosophy* to manage himself in the face of his final predicament. The first martyr of philosophy, Socrates (c. 470–399 BC), shows a similar if not greater resilience in the face of his own coming execution, except in his case it was philosophy that got him into trouble with his accusers in the first place. The radical Socrates found his peace in his principles such that for him, his death scarcely mattered. However, Socrates warns his killers that their trouble is only about to begin as his ends. They surely thought him extraordinarily odd for taking no more account for his life than to warn them about theirs.

## 1.2  The Place of Philosophy

A mistaken, though common perception of philosophy is that students must be dragged kicking and screaming to such a subject. Absent in such a judgment is acknowledgment that people have some natural inclination toward questions in life. Indeed, enough living inevitably brings people to even some of the questions of philosophy because life eventually ushers people toward questions wrongly presumed at first to have their sole origin in a classroom made miserable by an "introduction" to philosophy.

However, for those having little acquaintance with philosophers outside the classrooms of the Academy, it is easy to surmise that philosophy exists nowhere else but inside institutions of learning and for academic recluses who force their idea talk upon unwilling students. Philosophy appears as precisely the sort of subject having no concern with anything outside itself and a discipline invented by leisured and unimaginative academics living in the pampered Academy with nothing better to do than invent troublesome questions. Without the internal and artificial support lent by an institution for a subject largely absent in the real world, so the critic might charge, there might conceivably be neither philosophy nor philosophers in any world. Philosophy therefore may be presumed to exist because people in academic institutions create and maintain it, and since philosophy appears to be a subject that only thinks for the reward of thinking, it must find a safe haven to afford protection from the outside world. This haven is the required university as protecting mother. Thus, philosophers are almost exclusively tied to colleges and universities, where a subject having little to do with anything but itself can be protected while it is practiced.

This brief and hostile genealogy of philosophy makes no reference to the human anthropology giving rise to philosophy, while conveying the impression that the subject is as removed from life as anything could possibly be. However, philosophy is not always quartered inside the presumed artificial institution known as the Academy, but more to the point, philosophy is not clinging in death-averting dependence upon the Academy. Of course the Academy provides support for philosophy, but not unlike the way it does other fragile subjects, though the particular relationship it affords philosophy may be precisely for the kind of intellectual activity distinguished in philosophy. Moreover, the Academy does not support philosophy like a mother so fearful for a fragile child that the babe is never permitted to leave the hospital. In other words, philosophy may represent our most valiant and sustained attempt to interrogate and understand the world and ourselves. If that desire is not encouraged or protected, not only may philosophy be in jeopardy, but thinking for the sheer sake of knowing may falter and suffer abandon. Then the presumed distractions from living that the philosopher tempts us with might be silenced in being forsaken by the world.

All the same, the presence of philosophy in the Academy and its contended absence elsewhere can seem calculated to satisfy these few professional folks—the philosophers—for philosophy is a subject that seems so removed from ordinary life that it seems no surprise that it be quartered in an unordinary place for odd people. As mentioned earlier, though some of the negative perception of the philosopher is nervousness or intimidation before the philosophical ability, in most cases of indifference or hostility, there is resistance to philosophy perceived as spending so much time on so little, or worse, on nothing.

The life of philosophy, however, though developed and nurtured largely by stepping back from the world, might paradoxically be considered the most necessary skill for anyone living in the world. It might be the case that philosophy is the subject matter most natural to the university in order to train people for life. To accomplish this, people detour from "real" life for a few years in order to live "better" lives on their return to a real life not so unquestionable and therefore not so immoveable or invincible any more. Philosophy, like the larger university, represents the attempt to stand outside life for a time in order to understand life and the world better. Yet, the separation and independence of philosophy cast suspicions on philosophy as being integral to life. The separation veils one of the real purposes of philosophy, in the way that the university itself may also be thought of as a diversion from life.

Nevertheless, philosophy still looks like play time to many people and more like a spurious luxury than work for a real purpose. In a world needing as much effort as ours, time spent on philosophy appears to require an extraordinary justification, for mention of the word philosophy inevitably suggests to many spending or stealing valuable time to stretch out and do nothing. This kind of leisure is deemed permissible when one has taken care of other things or does not have many things to do—and so we associate such a time with the lives of children or the affluent. Tellingly, the practice of philosophy seems to necessitate that some of the same privileges we allow children be permitted philosophers, though philosophers can appear as less likeable adults when regurgitating some of the questions of the inquisitive child. Furthermore, we find some of the originators of Western philosophy, Plato and Aristotle for example, coming from families that had the leisure and opportunity to philosophize. Socrates apparently did not come from such a family; he is reputed to have been the son of a stonemason, but Socrates is as much given to the idea of knowledge for the sake of knowledge as any other higher-born philosopher.

While philosophy may connote the picture of a pastime unnecessary to real life, such a perspective obstructs the realization that philosophy and philosophical thinking may not be luxuries at all, but in fact necessities and that to refrain from philosophy because of the other business of life can be simply a diversion, or worse, an escape from life. It is a revealing observation of human nature that truth be told, we have time for those things for which we wish to have time. The hesitation of the university student toward philosophy, moreover, balks against a requirement to take a class in philosophy from a university that insures the student encounters the subject. The willing as well as the unwilling student must therefore spend some time in a subject that to most may appear of no use for life outside the Academy. The intent of the requirement, however, is to insure that no student leaves the university as the same student who entered because education is not for standing still or remaining the same but for growing. Nevertheless, the practical requirement from the begrudging student, the requirement that philosophy show its reason to be, is a sore point for students mandated to take such a subject. Thus, the teacher has to sell philosophy to students for the most part resistant to it, since it seems to them to lack a connection with the real world and real life.

The teacher may persuade the student that philosophy is everybody's business and that philosophy is not only or even a luxury but also a necessity. One way to do this is to show the philosophical assumptions and underpinnings in much of what we believe and take for granted. In this way, the teacher may intimate to the students doggedly resistant to philosophy that they are simply burying their heads in the sand. Of course, the students are probably enjoying life for the most part—except for philosophy class   and comfortable with their beliefs or lack of them, and perhaps fearful to examine some or any of them, for such scrutiny may cause them to rethink many things not given much thought before the encounter with philosophy.

Seen in this manner, philosophical thinking is paradoxically not encouraging a retreat from the real world, but an injunction to look at it. Until the student confronts this as his choice, he is apt to remain in retreat from philosophy. Thus, while philosophy may be visually seen only inside the Academy, it may be imminently usable on the outside. We may not, after all, be resistant to philosophy because it looks like wasteful play, but because we fear the hard work it demands. This being said, the justification of philosophy may not lie in what we can do with philosophy, but what it will do to us. In other words, we may be staying away from philosophy out of fear of knowing the truth that might be more discomforting than we would wish.

One may of course be more open to philosophy and the questions it raises at particular times of life, rather than others. As already mentioned, one might hazard that serious matters have a better reception among people during serious occasions of life, not unlike when people turn to religious faith or something similar when they experience grave crises. Moreover, people require the perception of a problem before they might turn attention to the problem. If philosophy can be disconcerting for those resisting its unwelcome intrusions, a willing audience may be those disconcerted or disillusioned persons looking for something. Those looking the least, by contrast, may have least chance of finding anything significant.

However, the abiding perception of philosophy will be that this discipline encompasses subject matter most removed from real life and therefore occupies the highest rung of the ivory tower of the university. The problems between students and philosophy no doubt beset the teaching of the humanities in general, as subject matter that students do not find imminently practical. Situated in the ivory tower, philosophy, however, may be perceived as the worst offender as it looks down and surveys life and the world, connoting an air of pompous presumption, with no apparent connection to anything but itself. The student after all may confront formal philosophy for the first time in the academic setting and will begin to suspect that a subject presumed found only inside the ivory tower is an indication of its irrelevance on the outside.

Socrates engaged in philosophical discussion in the public square and was well known as a philosopher without being part of an institution. In fact, he was an itinerant philosopher of sorts, given to moving freely about Athens. Socrates's contention that "The unexamined life is not worth living" gave a practical orientation to his philosophical pursuits that almost necessarily put him on the street and not in a school. Other philosophers of his day, called the Sophists, traveled more extensively than Socrates, though they were critiqued by Socrates because their philosophical positions often contradicted his own. By contrast, Plato, the student of Socrates, started a school with his Academy around 387 BC, and Aristotle, the student of Plato, founded his own school called the Lyceum a little later. Philosophy has thus been a subject in institutions of learning long before the present, but the presence of philosophy today seems limited to the university. This casts a long but deceptive shadow over philosophy suggesting that philosophy has nothing to do with life. Thus, the life of philosophy seems lived inside the university because that seems the only place where one may visually see philosophy and philosophers.

However, one may find philosophical issues considered without philosophers being present. That is, not finding a philosopher on main street the way one finds a dentist or a plumber or an accountant does not literally mean that people have absolutely no time or place for interests that we might justly deem philosophical. Philosophy may be found beneath an exterior that may disguise it. Life hardly guarantees exemption from difficulties and thus draws the living toward a search for some answers. If Thoreau was correct in his famous wording that "Most men lead lives of quiet desperation," then we can expect to see people grapple with such questions in various ways and forms, however subtle or blatant and certainly not all of them in the explicit context of philosophy. Moreover, if some of the issues of philosophy surface in life itself, then it is no surprise that various aspects of human life and culture contend or resonate with many pieces of the marrow of philosophy.

Religion in the "real" world—though not in general in the Academy—has more prestige and more influence than philosophy. Inside the Academy of today's world, that comparison favors philosophy, often to the point of a near reversal. Strident defenders of religion and philosophy therefore are sometimes fierce opponents of each other, suggesting that a consideration of religious beliefs is one origin of philosophical thinking—or perhaps the reverse. Probably some readers have been witness to the haranguing of philosophy from a pulpit or the blasting of religion from the lectern. This antagonism suggests that in some way philosophy and religion might be contending for some of the same ground and that their animosity toward each other is witness to such a competition.

The fact that some of philosophy's most notorious questions such as "Does life have a meaning?" are generally given answer by religion suggests the conflict between the two. However, perhaps it is the case that antagonism between them is simply because religion provides an answer to which philosophy asks a question. More extreme will be the case in which religion may announce it has no need of the question because it has the answer, and equally uncompromising the philosopher may contend that no answer to the question is possible. Certainly there is more to the conflict between the two than this; however, philosophy often presents the religious answer as simply false, whereas religion often surmises that the question of philosophy is designed to remain a question forever or that philosophy intentionally desires to discredit any answer of religion.

Another distinction of philosophy is apparent when comparing philosophy to these other components of our lives. That is, people hopeful for an answer will probably tend to cast their hopes more toward something with some promise of answers than toward philosophy, filled with doubts and multiplying questions. That is, when one consults a psychologist or a financial advisor or a home decorator or even a psychic, the intention is for some answer or aid to the problems or issues brought to these practitioners. Because oftentimes one wants resolution, the practice of philosophy as seeming to perpetually ask and provoke questions appears to offer little hope for those desiring an answer and probably adamant for a quick one. This difference between many other ventures and philosophy seems to indicate that philosophy is significantly dedicated and defined by debate unlike some of the competition, and therefore, of dubious or unknown value to persons insistent upon the answers that practice often demands and deadlines exact.

All the same, part of the problem of finding a philosopher working outside the Academy, so as to possibly vindicate the worthiness of the philosopher inside, is that the work of the philosopher would seem to be the search for philosophical wisdom, and this not unnaturally suggests to us the schoolish atmosphere that circumscribes the idea of philosophy as birthed and maintained and therefore confined to the Academy. I am reminded of a brief conversation I had with my dentist over this question when I was a graduate student in philosophy. In the desire to make some pleasant conversation, and on discovering my choice of profession as teaching philosophy, the dentist asked me if I would be able to do anything with philosophy but teach. I accepted his dim assessment of philosophy with some chagrin, but dared not offer an offending defense of my subject with the domineering dental instruments in my mouth. However, I mentioned the conversation to a sympathetic friend from the humanities later, and she suggested that I should have asked the dentist if he could do anything with dentistry besides work on people's teeth. Comparing occupations this way, it would seem people choosing a career exclude themselves from ventures other than those for which they are trained.

However, there is more about philosophy to consider beyond the dentist's dubious presumption that the trained philosopher is headed either to the classroom or to the unemployment line. After completing dental school, the dentist can work on the teeth of people, or he can teach people to work on people's teeth. Let us compare that to what a philosopher might do. A philosopher can, as my dentist suggested, teach others, but can he also "do" philosophy and what would this "doing philosophy" be doing? The apparent answer is that this "doing" is teaching, but that was the point of my dentist: philosophy seems to be a subject you can only teach to others.

Part of the recurrent problem is that, as mentioned earlier, philosophy has no physical product, like good teeth or telescopes or fastballs. The chief value of philosophy, however, may lie precisely in the fact that it provokes questions about life that the possession of good teeth or telescopes or fastballs would never raise. The value of philosophy may be that it does something that few other things do. Furthermore, philosophy may inspire questions that other areas of human knowledge would scarcely raise but for perpetually inquisitive questioners who multiply their questions in want of an answer. Philosophy may teach us not to live life on the surface, and that indeed the examined life is a good and prudent way to get the most from life. That undertaking may not be easy, but few things of extraordinary value in life are extraordinarily easy. This characteristic of philosophy may therefore make it valuable for life in a way that little else compares or therefore competes.

We might say that the value of philosophy for life is in what it gives to people, but this would be to mistake philosophy for something analogous to dental work. In other words, philosophy does something to people that provokes them to approach the world in a way different from a habit of mind that simply accepts the world as found. We can say that the practice of dentistry exists so as to ensure people of good teeth. We might also say that what philosophy gives to people is what philosophy does to people. Dental work is not analogous, because dental care does not change the person, but only the teeth, whereas philosophy has the capability of changing the human person. This of course can make philosophy sound like religion or therapy, and though such a suggestion may sound offensive to practitioners of these professions perceiving the contrasting features of each, to state the matter this way also makes philosophy seem scary—and indeed it can be scary. However, as a student once said to me, philosophy will cease to be evaluated as scary after it is seen to be necessary. Moreover, whether we go to philosophy or not, philosophy eventually comes to us. This is to say again that life prods us at least on occasion to think philosophically, though we may resist the impulse for a time, but hopefully not for a lifetime. Seen in this light, philosophy can be a life partner.

Philosophy, however, can shake things up that are shakable and push us to consider matters that never mattered before we awaken from inattentive lives. Although a philosophical education can build confidence in the human mind and in the human person, that same confidence must be tempered in being subjected to the boundaries and challenges of truth. In other words, philosophy may enlarge us on the one hand but severely discipline us on the other. Thus, philosophy does change those who study it, because philosophy attempts to see the world or reality or truth as it is, to get it right, and thus, get to the truth of the matter with no stipulations or reservations set up in advance to govern or hide or ignore what is found. The journey may be fearful and unwelcoming for some. Thus, the education of a person by philosophy, however enthralling it may be initially, can in fact also humble and not infrequently strain and sometimes rebuke the human confidence gained from such study. Because the freedom of philosophy is not a freedom to believe whatever one likes or wishes, the human made larger by the stretching of philosophical inquiry may also find great courage and resilience required. The philosopher can withstand even this ordeal, however, if he is committed to the injunction that there is scarcely ever any good reason not to know the truth, whatever it may be.

**Name:** _____          **Date:** _____

1. Why does the philosopher typically regard the world with a sense of puzzlement and is the philosopher justified in his puzzlement about the world?

2. What characteristics of a philosopher are apt to perhaps strengthen or weaken him in his relationships with people and the world around him?

# Chapter 2

# Philosophy as a Life

## 2.1 Philosophy as More than Life

Antagonism toward philosophy possibly reflects a negative impression of the demeanor of the philosopher toward the goal of inquiry, namely truth. That is, the philosopher may seem too aggressive or even couched with pride. However, these appearances may be in part because the philosopher counts on truth as robust. This means the philosopher presumes truth is not of a sort that one needs fear for it, for such a suspicion would reflect poorly upon one's conception of truth. Rather, one should be resolute with inquiries, content that for as long as we strive to eliminate bias and aspire to fairness and objectivity in questioning, inquiry should present no adverse risk or threat. Moreover, defenders of a position who are uneasy over any scrutiny may be doubtful rather than confident of the position protected. That is, if one must tip-toe in the consideration of truth, then the suspicion of falsity may be as likely as the presumption of the truth. Without questions being permitted, an answer seems remote.

From the perspective of the critic of philosophy, however, the practice and posture of philosophers seems bound to unravel our world. Viewed this way, the philosopher is deemed a radical trouble-maker and poised in a vain and prideful posture toward the world. However, as noted earlier, the inquisitive philosopher also resembles a curious child wanting answers to questions, even though the adult questioner encounters far less sympathy and likely provokes serious reaction with his troublesome questions.

The philosopher, nevertheless, wants to get at the truth, despite the tumult his inquiry may provoke. The truth of the matter is that this habit of philosophy has and always will be irritating to someone and most probably to many. Plato spoke of the "ancient quarrel between poetry and philosophy" in his time, while Aristophanes (c. 448–385 BC), the Athenian playwright, mocked at Socrates lulling about Athens poised with questions, while the irritated Athenians recoiled and eventually struck back at Socrates. Aristotle, after perceiving the escalating ire between Macedonia and Greece, retreated to his homeland in Macedonia "lest Athens sin twice against philosophy." The irritation toward philosophers is not a recent or only a modern phenomenon. It is ages old; indeed, it is as old as philosophy itself. This is to say that philosophy provokes irritation for a good number because it can be upsetting.

To practitioners, philosophy at times requires more than simply a good or strong mind, for something of a substantial stomach in the form of intellectual courage is needed. That is, living the life of philosophy can create the anxiety of wondering whether rest is anywhere in a future with philosophy. In short, a certain fortitude and resilience seems required for the aspirant submitting to the philosophical quest. A venture of this kind can make philosophy seem scary to many, for here the innocence and purity of philosophy recedes and is replaced by some inevitable anxiety. Unlike the exuberant wonder of the young child anxious to find out about his world, the adult philosopher is uneasy about what may be the result of his reason and his searches. All of this is to say that we may hesitate before submitting to the life of philosophy, fearing its judgments of our lives and our ways. Indeed, it may appear that philosophy as a life jeopardizes life. Philosophy may seem to take people from the comforts of the world, which nevertheless may be eerily feared to perhaps not be the real world.

Iris Murdoch (1919–1999), the late novelist and philosopher, claimed that philosophy inevitably makes people anxious because it positions people between two worlds. Murdoch writes:

> I think philosophy is very counter-natural, it is a very odd unnatural activity. Any teacher of philosophy must

feel this. Philosophy disturbs the mass of semi-aesthetic conceptual habits on which we normally rely. Hume said that even the philosopher, when he leaves his study, falls back on these habitual assumptions. . . . It is an attempt to perceive and to tease out in thought our deepest and most general concepts. It is not easy to persuade people to look at the level where philosophy operates.

Murdoch is pointing to the resistance involved in permitting philosophy to join one's life. Though productive philosophy requires some smarts, and while others may be somewhat admiring of the intellect of the philosopher—though probably at some safe and calculated distance—the greater difficulty in the practice of the discipline, however, is where philosophy may leave us. We can be left very unsettled so that we may desire to flee after the first challenge. Philosophy changes us, but first, and for some time, it unsettles us. When we break from it, we escape from the exertion it places us under and return to a cozier world we are frankly glad to see and to embrace again. David Hume (1711–1776), the modern Scottish philosopher, wrote about the welcome consolation of the parlor after the frightfulness of a philosophical study. Why? Because the ordinary way we look at the world seems up for question in philosophy and with it our comfort and familiar way of looking at that world and ourselves. Study of both can be frightful with philosophy as a guide. We may ask, then, why should we do this to ourselves?

Plato's *Allegory of the Cave* illustrates something of this dilemma and the results of taking and not taking the fork in the road toward examination of the self and the world. Plato's story starts among a group of people we might imagine as ourselves, even though the setting of his story is one where prisoners in a cave, with their hands chained behind them, are only able to see what is to their front. Behind them, moreover, is a fire providing for some needed warmth and light. Because of the light cast by the fire, anything from behind the prisoners but in front of the fire casts a shadow on the cave wall in front of the prisoners. The prisoners, never seeing the objects behind them, but only the shadows in front, understandably presume that the shadows are independent objects. One day, however, one prisoner manages to break free of his chains and gropes his way out and to the mouth of the cave, where he encounters and witnesses the extraordinary light of the sun. With this new revelation, he now surmises that the shadows of the cave were simply that, shadows. Because this is not a trival bit of information, he then feels a responsibility to return to the cave to enlighten his peers about their deluded conception of the world. However, his fellow prisoners grow annoyed with his explanation of their state, and after some sparing with the returning prisoner, they end up killing him to shut him up.

The story clearly parallels the life and death of Socrates and is one motive of Plato in constructing such a tale. In other words, the philosopher is not likely to receive any ovations from hearers; he is more likely to be rejected. Moreover, in the actual details of Socrates's life, we see a philosopher who amazingly seems unruffled by the deadly reception accorded him, even after he has been something of a public intellectual, if not in fact a public servant, for decades. Furthermore, during the trial of Socrates, he manifests an almost incomprehensible lack of concern for his life before accusers intent to silence him for good. He exhibits remarkable courage in the face of these antagonists, who are made to look by Socrates as if it is they and not he who should be on trial. This despite the fact that Socrates's accusers undoubtedly wanted him out of the way after his orations against them—and quickly out of the way to save them any further embarrassment.

In Socrates we thus have a person amply living the life of philosophy to the very end of his life. Most astounding about him is how he endures under conditions that most people would find too taxing in requiring more courage than they possess. That is, everything that could possibly be against Socrates is lodged against him, and yet he manages death without a trace of trauma and with a sobering calmness hardly suggestive of any calamity at all. Despite some irresponsible accusers taking his life from him, the perplexity of Socrates's willingness to give his life to them and maybe for them has evoked reactions of amazement across the centuries. It is little wonder that later medieval religious philosophers would see in the example of Socrates a prototype of Christ.

Most of us, however, never rise to the stature of Socrates' courage, for we are in varying degrees reasonably content in something like Plato's cave. There we live with unquestioned shadows and all seem content with the restive and enjoyable experience of what we have. Here we escape the penetrating gaze of the sun upon our condition and world by not moving from the comforting fire to the brighter light of illumination. Life is usually jolted after a stint in the study or the revealing light because of the realization that philosophy can change the way we live, for philosophy changes the manner we look at ourselves and the world. Life, or ordinary life, therefore, often resists such an intrusion. The Shadow has a comfort found lacking when the sun shows the shadow for what it is. The critical aspect of philosophy questions so much of our ordinary world that it sends many potential philosophers scurrying away. Seen in this vein, the person who advances into the sobering world of philosophy requires some stamina to remain steadfast in the face of a surprising new world. For in the study—unlike existence in the cave or the parlor— the philosopher peels away the layers of concepts we have woven into our world of unquestioning habit. Peeling some layers of muddled and largely unthinking accretions away, the philosopher comes upon a new world that the inquirer might greet with revulsion or repression but also perhaps relief. The stalwart philosopher, however, can accommodate an apprehensive uncomfortableness by his earnest resolution to discern the truth.

Therefore, the initial impression we may receive from philosophy is nervousness over how much philosophy can change us. Philosophy might humble us, if we get too close by conceding its relevance to a life previously lived without it. Philosophy, in a word, can be rough on us. However, this is simply to say that we may fear how poorly we might fare under the scavenging eyes of reason, most especially when we have never bothered to look upon ourselves and our world in this new manner until now.

This sort of initial torture within the gauntlet of philosophy, however, is not the whole story, but alas, it is where most of us must begin. This means that for the most part, we are walking around as strangers to ourselves and the world and with fearful apprehensions of what may turn up if we make significant acquaintance with questions about both. Stating the matter this way forces us to confront the sobering realization that we are inside a body and a world in which we have perhaps little to no stake because both were built before us and without us. Thus, we scarcely know who we are or what anything might be.

For sure we may rattle off our so-called accidents of birth, but we know that with them glaring at us, we did not pick them, though they have fashioned us. This realization can be a memorable dismembering of the human person with the humbling admission that we have been living under someone else's piloting. This passenger may now want to fly his own plane, but he lacks experience. He is understandably nervous under the dawning realization that we have not built ourselves in any meaningful sense of that term. Rather, we inherit ourselves. Moreover, as philosophers we desire to become consciously aware of our inheritance, so that as thinking people we can interact with it rather than being dominated or blinded by it, nor unappreciative of it. To live without ever weighing in on ourselves is to approach our life and world rather blindly, by simply picking up from where we are put down. This means that we may presume a whole mass of beliefs about life that have been inherited by a self and world we are now mulling over.

To contemplate this change may seem a most excruciating kind of experience for an individual to have, but it also represents the kind of awakening that may give rise to an introduction to a lifelong friend called philosophy. Some philosophical starts may have had their birth in flights of imagination that initially at least were accompanied with much extraordinary and appealing intellectual satisfaction. But the difficult trials of philosophy can put ordinary life on hold for a time for some, until the individual recuperates by finding his way toward some anchors providing him courage enough to start looking with eyes open, no matter how daunting that task. Philosophy is the attempt to see ourselves and the world as they are. As logical as this seems, it is a path not usually traversed without some trepidation.

This is to say that an introduction to philosophy may be jolting to life for a time. In other words, marriage to philosophy may prove immensely satisfying given enough time, but the honeymoon, which comes first, may be less than comforting. Life may hit bottom in such experiences because of the realization that we are, for the most part, foreigners to the person and the world we occupy. In other words, we need to now get acquainted with what we only presumed to know earlier. That experience can be jarring, but it need not be lasting because it can act as propellant to find out about ourselves and our world. With the maze of beliefs held before, we may have lived well or even happily, or so we thought. This new way of living now seems to make life more difficult.

Moreover, there are reasons making life lived with philosophy appear as if life will never recover again. Most noticeable is that such an experience of diving into philosophy appears to confront a sea of perpetual uncertainty. If this predicament is prolonged or festers, permanent skepticism may result, where staying on the stairs produces atrophy because one fears never finding a true or sufficient landing. That is, the realization of a host of possible solutions to a single problem multiplied by many such problems and a myriad of responses to each problem can be daunting to someone trying to put feet down in the correct place amidst a plethora of places to land. As a student of mine once perceptively wrote, philosophy has none of the answers, but it has all of the questions.

However, this perception can evoke a mistaken impression to the newcomer to philosophy—that is, that philosophers are forever undecided on every question ever raised as proved by the fact that the questions continue to be raised. It is largely true that as a subject, philosophy rarely definitely settles the issues it scrutinizes, but individual philosophers do contend for positions taken and argue for them at length and with passion. This is to say that though the discipline of philosophy creates the appearance of only questions and no answers, individual philosophers maintain and defend positions they deem as no less defensible even though not every thinker agrees with their stance.

Skeptics there are among philosophers, though generally they are in the minority, albeit sometimes their influence is out of proportion to their relatively small numbers. In our day, too, a renewed argument comes from postmodernists touting the morality of suspending judgment. So of course philosophy, constantly sorting and making judgments historically, is judged ever so severely. One argument of the postmodernist is that the prestige of truth propelling the pursuit of truth is ultimately dangerous, simply because it pridefully provokes the notion of being correct. This mistaken inquiry, so the postmodernist claims, evokes debate producing a decision deemed correct and thus vilifying others as incorrect. The net result is one of domination and intolerance that begets difficulty for dissidents deemed mistaken. At the same time, those conversations that issue this kind of presumptuous thought for themselves produce a cultural stifling of the "other."

This charge, however, is a curious argument, claiming as it does, that the traditional goal of thought as truth creates too much hurt when we say or decide too much. To axiomize this belief, truth is conceived, not as robust, but as relative, though here the postmodern relativist defends his argument for relativism with robustness nearly equivalent to the older notion of the robustness of truth. This critic, therefore, encourages all sorts of chatter, each as good as the chatter of a neighbor next door or across the sea, coupled with the axiom that the tendency to judgment should be checked as we open our ears to a sea of positions in the interest of bringing no offense to any. To embrace this notion, however, is to abandon the traditional goal of philosophers trying to sort out the best arguments for the positions taken. To the degree that some present-day philosophers embrace it, they have given up, for the most part, on the notion of philosophy as evaluative for the notion of philosophy as simply or only listening. They imply and insist that nothing is "correct." The dangerous part of this kind of philosophical morality is in how its presumed moral superiority imperils any true judgments judged as arrogant for the presumed immorality of making a judgment.

Even if one avoids the emptiness of the postmodern turn, however, philosophy may produce or evoke little of the jubilant wonderment of the child discovering his world. That is, the adult questioner by contrast may have the premonition that truth is always closer to a frown than a smile. Therefore, pessimistic conclusions are temptingly viewed as closer to truthful conclusions, because these are thought to be the necessary attendant of truth. The not infrequent and sometimes humorless seriousness of the philosopher provides some understanding of this perception of philosophy.

However, the visitor or newcomer to philosophy may avoid conjecturing what kind of landing he is apt to make once he commits to philosophy. To some readers this kind of assurance may seem peculiar and perhaps implies that one is to take on faith that philosophy will aid rather than harm the individual. However, philosophy wants to get to the bottom of things and in going to the bottom, it is almost necessarily going to upset something. Traditional philosophy wants to see things clearly, as opposed to hazily. It prefers light or knowledge to darkness or shadows or ignorance or the postmodern judgment that no judgments are allowed. Philosophy tries hard to assume neutrality or objectivity in the desire to make sense of problems. This procedure should enable some understanding of the manner in which philosophy works to those perplexed by the methods or the presumed arrogance of philosophers. That is, philosophy is not by definition defiant or haughty, but it is as uncompromising as possible in turning over every stone and trying to get down to things believed real and true. Moreover, when we remind ourselves that the goal of inquiry is to ascertain and get acquainted with what is real and true, trepidation should retract a bit, for this may be—and indeed many times is—an arduous journey, but philosophers deem the promise worth the peril. Just as truth has nothing to fear from honest inquiry, so too we should have nothing to fear from truth.

This "bottom of things" is sometimes referred to as "foundationalism" by philosophers. This is a term suggesting that there is a landing that philosophical inquirers can in time come to rest upon and even uniformly work from. This foundation is sometimes said to be the laws of logic, such as the principle of identity. In pursuit of truth from here, therefore, this philosopher is not trying to reconstitute the world but rather to understand its constitution.

## 2.2 Philosophy as Less than Life

Philosophy appears to some to constitute a retraction from real life, especially when we consider how it might turn our lives around. This means that the objector might think that the thinking and inclinations of the philosopher pull one away from reality toward a world of theory and speculation and abstraction that diminish the extent to which a philosopher can be a man or woman of the world. Said this way, it may appear that to be a philosopher, one must renounce the world in the intent to understand it. Here again the aspiring philosopher seems pulled between two worlds.

The endeavor and enterprise of philosophy is not, however, an undertaking ultimately alien to the human person. Aristotle in fact claimed that the human species has its identity in the use of reason and that the human is most felicitous when reasoning. Indeed, for Aristotle, inasmuch as God is seen as "Thought thinking itself," we are, according to Aristotle, most like God when we are thinking. In what may look like a self-aggrandizing move by a philosopher touting philosophy, Aristotle nevertheless implies that the philosopher is the human most advancing his humanity in practicing philosophy. In another manner of speaking, moreover, Aristotle is conceding that reasoning is what humans do *qua humans*—that is, our most distinctive identity is not precisely our physical machinery or our laboratories or any of our stuff but our reason, which made all these things and more possible. The creature who is human is most human when he thinks. Indeed, he cannot keep from thinking and reasoning, for thinking is in his blood, so to speak. Or, as J.H. Randall Jr. (1899–1980), a notable historian of philosophy, wrote boldly of philosophy, "She belongs to the oldest profession in the world: she exists to give men pleasure, and to satisfy their imperious needs."

Philosophy, however, is perhaps most about self-democracy, however unfriendly or intimidating it may look in the beginning. For philosophy makes us aware of how much we can take charge of ourselves. It can make life less scary because it charges us to take ownership of ourselves in the spirit of a deliberate discipline that instills in us a pointed sense of purpose or control. However, because the philosopher is committed to truth, the freedom one finds is not the abandonment of responsibility or allegiance, but the willingness to consider ourselves and our world from its vantage point. In this way, life is a project for philosophy, so that philosophy is not taking from life but supporting it.

To a certain extent the negative observation about the life of the philosopher or the philosophically inclined person taking away from life is true. Nevertheless, to understand something requires some study of that something—life included. To live life at its fullest is to understand life. There is thus no absolute dichotomy between living and studying. The raising of questions is built into the fabric of life, for neither questions nor philosophy first originate with the academic philosopher going to a podium in a classroom inside a building. Therefore, the studiousness of the philosopher is not simply or only a bookish study confined to a desk and chair, but an inquisitiveness that attends most everything in life.

The critic of philosophy may nevertheless express hesitation that the philosopher seems obsessively committed to a kind of thought that the critic may find perplexing or downright dreadful. In other words, the habit of study is sure to diminish one's relationship to the world around him because it distances one from that world. One trades one's life for philosophy when one takes up with philosophy for life, so the charge might say. This kind of complaint serves to remind us, however, how much requirements in virtually anything demand of us. I remember once hearing an Olympic runner being told by an adoring fan that she would give her life to be able to run like the Olympic runner, to which the Olympian replied that she had. To be fair, I have also heard Olympian athletes admit they often desire to live something of a more normal life. This desire follows simply because the amount of time in training tended to remove the disciplined athlete from much else she wanted to do. The improving of ordinary life to live an extraordinary life comes with a price that confers something of a privilege that few people aspire to attain.

The question of costs or price might turn upon something of a cost–benefits analysis. In such an analysis one might look to evaluate whether the prize is worth the punishment, which means of course that one is hopeful that what one gets exceeds what one gives. While this sort of computational exchange might appropriately describe a financial transaction or trade or even a job change or maybe a choice of profession, it seems extraordinarily weak when applied to decisions about how we should live. Does our final commitment to who we are and how we live come down to what makes us perspire the least?

We might begin to answer this question by considering if we extend our support or allegiance or effort to some things largely irrespective of the degree of difficulty? Of course we do, and these are the things that typically matter most to us, as evidenced by the fact that our commitments to them sometimes know no bounds. Typically too, many of those things tend not to be material things. Said another way, material things often are subjected to cost–benefit analysis; the things that matter more are less typically evaluated this way. What makes for the difference? One might conjecture that they give different kinds of happiness or satisfaction or affirm human identity differently.

To consider this point, we can enlist part of a philosophical dispute involving the British Utilitarians of the nineteenth century. They contended that the kind of life and actions humans should engage in amounts to the question of identifying those things providing for human happiness or satisfaction. John Stuart Mill (1806–1873), one of the most prominent utilitarians, however, was not content to simply identify any and every good as producing happiness of a generic kind without any distinctions among them. Mill instead contended for a differentiation among the various things providing for human happiness. His point was the obvious one that some happiness is a better or stronger kind and thus will be more desired. Mill thought that this was vindicated in actual human experience, for he argued that the distinction made among types of happiness was evident in our experience. In other words, if some kinds of happiness are greater than others, all other things being equal, the difference should be discernible to and among people experiencing the myriad kinds of happiness. That is, a claimed distinction should show a real difference.

Mill thus believed that some satisfactions are worthier of more effort and struggle than others. In fact, Mill had to go further and argue that his philosophy that held up satisfaction and happiness as the rightful goals of ethical choices was not, as some of his critics charged, a rank hedonism incapable of producing martyrs, for example. To make this point and to argue also the prior point that some pleasures are more ultimately gratifying than others, Mill evoked the contrast between very different kinds of goods in his contention that "It is better to be a human being dissatisfied than a pig satisfied; better to be Socrates dissatisfied than a fool satisfied." In the comparison one observes that what we might term ordinary satisfaction or happiness of a material kind may even appear remote or absent from the higher happiness. That is, though Socrates's principles proved to be stronger than his predicament, his victory produces neither ovation nor jubilation, but indeed in many ways portends the opposite— the pain and loss of Socrates's death. It is, nevertheless, the right and noble thing to do according to Mill. In trying to answer the question of how could this be, we may shed some light on our previous consideration of how the extraordinary Socrates managed the kind of courage evidenced at his trial and execution.

The critic may ask, however, where is this line of reasoning headed? In other words, how can we bear the burden of thinking the principles we should live by are in effect higher than our own life, as Mill's preference for the actions of Socrates suggests? Stated another way, is there something to which we owe allegiance, such that we should continue in that allegiance, even when embracing it is inconvenient or painful or even deadly?

Stated negatively, can we imagine anything that is worth the price of life? Stated this way, however, we may presume the point is entirely negative. Thus, we might ask, as we sometimes hear it put: can we imagine anything worth the cost of death. If not, however, we may be reduced to simply existing and trying to keep our existence going for the sake of existing. In other words, if the only reason we are left with is the preservation of ourselves for the sake of preservation, then some form of hedonism may be our reigning philosophy of life, though by default and not by design. Bertrand Russell made something of this point in a poignant passage from his book *The Principles of Social Reconstruction*:

> The world has need of a philosophy, or a religion, which will promote life. But in order to promote life it is necessary to value something other than mere life. Life devoted only to life is animal, without any real human value, incapable of preserving men permanently from weariness and the feeling that all is vanity. If life is to be fully human it must serve some end which seems, in some sense, outside human life, some end which is impersonal and above humankind, such as God or truth or beauty. Those who best promote life do not have life for their purpose. They aim rather at what seems like a gradual incarnation, a bringing into our human existence of something eternal, something that appears to imagination to live in a heaven remote from strife and failure and the devouring jaws of Time.

Therefore, the best life may not be the easiest life, and indeed it is difficult to imagine cases where it would be. This is because most of us require some work to make ourselves into the kind of person we feel reasonably accepting of, surmising that we are not living life fully if we are simply or exclusively living with and for mundane and material comforts. Russell's notion of the way to live, however, might be in the minority, when, as example, narcissist behaviors can be observed in plentiful quantity. So too, a society making leisure possible may lurch culturally downward. However, the life of leisure that many crave is also a condition usually necessary for the higher things of civilization and produces many of our cultural gems and indeed many of our philosophers of note. Moreover, we seldom find extraordinary work done when cultures are in decline, for it usually requires something of an advancing rather than a declining civilization to produce extraordinary people, and this usually requires leisure, or to put it in the vernacular, time off. That is, thought and brilliant thought are apt to be significantly less exercised in periods of social instability, because while turbulence in life can provoke an individual to some hard but genuine thinking about life that an easy life might never gain, it is also the case that an element of idleness put to good use is usually necessary for truly extraordinary achievements.

It is, therefore, no accident that Western philosophy first arises and for a season flourishes exceedingly where Western democracy also first arises—in Greece. Nor is it surprising that Plato and Aristotle came from well-to-do families in ancient Greece. Plato's family had been involved in Athens politics for some time, though Plato soured on politics and particularly despised Athenian democracy after the execution of his teacher Socrates. Aristotle's father was physician to Philip of Macedonia, and Aristotle himself was the tutor of the youthful son of Philip, the later famed Alexander the Great. Socrates, as an exception, was reputed to be the son of a stonemason, with none of the blue-blood lineages of the aforementioned Greek philosophers. Both Plato and Aristotle started their own schools, and undoubtedly their students came from the upper tiers of Greek society as did their teachers. However, the student reading these pages may resent the nearly forced exposure to philosophy in the classroom that his material gains (or that of his parents) afford him. The difference we might first explain as the thirst for wisdom being eclipsed as the necessities of food, clothing, and shelter are acquired. However, there is no necessity in this, even though it seems a reasonable historical surmise concerning the modern Western world. Said another way, wealth and wisdom need not only be found in a combination where one negates the other. Plato and Aristotle certainly possessed the required material necessities for maintenance of material life and yet remained diligent in the quest for wisdom. So maybe the differences among people are somewhat ahistorical with reference to individuals, rather than people or persons simply being historically conditioned.

We might consider the question in the broader context of cultures where we could find a different experience than that of the modern Western world. That is, the materialist answer of Western modernity may hold strong sway over Western culture to the point that matters of wisdom are given little attention after material wealth is achieved. However, in Eastern cultures, by and large, the two presumed incompatibles of Western culture are much more joined. That is, the East has tended to regard life as more of a whole, with the compartmentalization of life and knowledge somewhat foreign to them. Confucius (551–479 BC), for example, in effect saw education as the meaning of life. By this he meant that life was a time for unceasing learning until we ceased to live, which should mean at the time of death. He would inevitably think the idea of bracketing higher education to four years was arbitrary and showed an ignorance of the necessity of knowledge for life. The person of wisdom or the sage in Eastern culture is given much prestige, whereas in Western culture, particularly American culture, which is identifiably among the most materialistically oriented cultures of the West, the intellectual is somewhat suspect. In the East even the ordinary person on average will tend to appreciate and revere "deep questions" more than his Western counterpart, who is typically impatient with such questions. The Westerner, moreover, takes such questions as largely divorced from life, by which is meant real life, by which is usually meant material life.

The Westerner, however, may think that life and the world are to be enjoyed, and distractions from that enjoyment are to be minimized. One rightly suspects that presumed in an argument of this kind is a conception of life at variance with much that philosophy requires. This is simply because philosophy prods us to consider living life on something of a higher plane. The objection, however, seems to be that life as life should be a relatively stable endeavor and things that come along to challenge our desire to live peaceably and comfortably may compromise our happiness. Living should not be interrupted by cumbersome or protracted questions about life, the life lived for ordinary happiness might say. However, this was precisely the argument we confronted in the beginning of this chapter. That is, the kind of questions philosophy poses for us may not even be good for us.

This point of view is fairly common not only among ordinary people but is one shared and sometimes insisted upon by notable Western intellectuals. As example, the famous psychoanalyst Sigmund Freud (1856–1939) wrote in a letter to his daughter, Anna, that "The minute a man ask himself the meaning of life he is sick." From the perspective on philosophy as presented in these pages, however, we might say no. Indeed, we would want to say that such a person has woken up from his slumbers, rather than routing himself toward compromises with his sanity. Thus, the student suspicious of philosophy may not have only the company of his peers in his critique of philosophy. He may also find his complaints shared by various intellectuals and even among some faculty at his university. Some of the significant criticisms of philosophy from other intellectuals must therefore be considered.

**Name:** _____          **Date:** _____

1. In what ways are people naturally philosophers and in
   what ways is philosophy unnatural to people?

2. In what ways might philosophy compromise a full life and in what ways might it enrich a life?

# Chapter 3

# The Persistence of Philosophy

## 3.1 The Rationalism of Philosophy

The student in philosophy class mesmerized with the subject makes no demand that philosophy connect with any "real" world. Such a student does not grow impatient in the philosophy classroom, nor is he disdainful toward the philosophy teacher enunciating the mistakes of ordinary thinking about the real world that other and uninterested students assume. This rare student offers attention while the teacher casts doubts on the dubious real world with effective questions that bore other listeners. This student is proof that the idea of knowledge for the sake of knowledge is possible and flourishing even in an age of distracting technology.

Although few students share in this kind of adulation of philosophy, vindicating the existence of a subject seemingly so distant from the vaunted real world is relatively easy for the teacher. This is done despite all the self-doubt present in some doubting philosophers and for all the disdain of this subject wielded by unwilling students. The usual attempt consists of reversing the presumed dichotomy between theory and practice by showing the dependence of practice on theory, and in this way exhibiting in undeniable manner that scrutiny with a critical eye toward the world is obligatory for thinking people. Examples to illustrate this contention are not difficult to find. Locke's famous treatises on government had to be conceived in thought for Jefferson and others to birth a real nation from it. Thus, Marx's memorable statement that the point of things is not to understand the world but to change it is depicted as woefully mistaken. One cannot, after all, make for meaningful change without understanding the nature of what is to be changed. The vindication of thinking philosophically about the real world follows a self-evident truth of logic.

However, for most students, their familiar world invites them back after sitting bored but tethered in a mandatory philosophy class. In other words, the comfort that comes from living in an assumed world is less laborious than watching reality critiqued by the philosopher with his logical tools. Although philosophy may strip away the surface and even some admittedly superficial layers of an object or belief, what remains may seem uninteresting or at least strange.

But most importantly, the project of philosophy can upend the interested and hopeful student who had some expectation of questions being clarified and maybe even resolved in philosophy class. However, an analysis by an instructor that is reductionist as a modern philosophical analysis might be, for example, can bewilder this student into thinking that how philosophy works will not work for him. That is, the student may observe that the philosopher habitually wants to corner the object or belief in all its nakedness, or foundation, or logical form, or essence, as the philosopher is apt to say. To the student, however, this translation may transform the subject or object into something almost diminutive or outlandish or even comical. Some of the most vocal critics of philosophers, moreover, have often portrayed this analytic tendency of philosophers as one of narrow rationalism, an example being provided in a well-known letter of the English poet John Keats (1795–1821), where he writes:

> The Imagination may be compared to Adam's dream—
> he awoke and found it truth. I am the more zealous in
> this affair, because I have never yet been able to perceive
> how anything can be known by consequitive reasoning—
> and yet it must be—Can it be that even the greatest
> Philosopher ever arrived at his goal without putting aside
> numerous objections—However it may be, O for a Life of
> Sensations rather than of Thoughts!

Keats is indicting philosophers as people who live in their heads while composing abstractions and reducing the complexity of the world to logical links as they depict reality in a nexus of sparkling but pointless reasoning. Moreover, Keats's larger point is that philosophers have missed and lost something in the substitution of cerebral machinations for material sensations and interactions; logic has absconded with their life and reduced their picture of the world and reality to a thought. This criticism extends to say that philosophers with their abiding rationalism do not have the whole but rather only a portion of the human person or the problem cornered in focus. D.H. Lawrence (1885–1930), in an essay "Why the Novel Matters," portrays the propensity of the philosopher and other offenders to go off the road and charges each with truncating something vital:

> And as for the sum of all knowledge, it can't be anything more than an accumulation of all the things I know in the body, and you, dear reader, know in the body. These damned philosophers, they talk as if they suddenly went off in steam, and were then much more important than they are when they're in their shirts. It is nonsense. Every man, philosopher included, ends in his own finger tips. . . . It seems impossible to get a saint, or a philosopher, or a scientist, to stick to this simple truth. They are all, in a sense, renegades. The saint wishes to offer himself up as spiritual food for the multitude. . . . The philosopher, on the other hand, because he can think, decides that nothing but thoughts matter. It is as if a rabbit, because he can make little pills, should decide that nothing but little pills matter. As for the scientist, he has absolutely no use for me so long as I am man alive. To the scientist, I am dead. He puts under the microscope a bit of dead me, and calls it me.

This kind of criticism of philosophy has some history and stems from the perspective that philosophers carry out analysis with eyes half shut from critically filtered lenses. This is surely a serious complaint against philosophy or philosophical method and warrants directing some attention to it, especially as some philosophers have sometimes made such a charge against other philosophers. One example from the twentieth century was A.N. Whitehead (1861–1947), the British philosopher. Whitehead was insistent that philosophy should remove no more from our perception of the world than science had already taken. Therefore, he attempted some compromise of the hard distinction between primary and secondary qualities found in science and was critical of the notion of the material world as composed, somewhat like Lawrence, of only "dead matter." He, like the French thinker Bergson (1859–1941), sought to escape the thoroughgoing mechanistic explanations of reality commonly found in their day. Other and earlier thinkers had made similar criticisms about other blind spots of philosophers. Nietzsche (1844–1900), for example, argued against Socrates's rationalism, by claiming that this philosopher was bereft of an esthetic element in his life and philosophy and that only pondering death gave him pause to needfully request some of Aesop's fables, something neglected beforehand. The remorseless rationalism in the upbringing of John Stuart Mill provoked Mill to an early breakdown at age 20, and even Sigmund Freud, mentioned earlier, wrote of the fact that the poets as prescient thinkers had thought his ideas before they were set out as belated Freudian discoveries. One common theme among such examples is that a rational lens bends or even distorts the way the philosopher sees the world—to include himself.

The controversy between Rene Descartes (1596–1650), called the Father of Modern Philosophy, and Blaise Pascal (1623–1662) illustrates one thinker accusing the other of being blind sighted by reason. Descartes wanted to put philosophy on a new footing and proceeded with a new methodical rigor designed to get to the truth, while also disarming his opponents along the way. With skeptics as his immediate antagonists, Descartes desired to establish and guard certainty against a renewed assault on reason from the skeptics of his day, who claimed that any and all knowledge was debatable and therefore doubtable. Part of Descartes' ploy was to assume the role of his opponent so as to prove the opponent's position untenable. Thus, he combats skepticism with skepticism and passionately looks the part of a skeptic in his maneuvering. Moreover, while proceeding to doubt everything, he reflects that when he is done, he nevertheless cannot doubt that he is doubting, and this realization ultimately leads to his famous quip, "I think, therefore I am."

However, Descartes's characterization of the human person as ultimately an immaterial thinking self provokes the kind of charge from Pascal that we heard from Lawrence. That is, Pascal charges that Descartes has missed part of the human person in Descartes's squeezed and truncated notion of the self. For Pascal there is a distortion of the object by the philosopher who relies only upon his keen reason—the long-standing tool of the philosopher at work—and perhaps ignores or simply misses any consequences of the limitations or peculiarities of reason contorting the subject or object subjected to the philosopher's reason.

Pascal's questioning of the rationalistic method in philosophy is reflected in his famous declaration that "the heart has reasons which reason knows nothing of." Pascal is asserting that the reason touted by the philosopher may miss some of the picture, or the reality, studied. Here the philosopher is called into question because his method is deemed questionable or evaluated as only partially successful for describing the subject or object. Since method is more definitive of philosophy than content, this criticism of philosophy may incessantly badger and make defensive the proponents of reason.

The contention over the possible limitations of reason extends to wider intellectual and cultural circles between rationalists (as expected, chiefly populated by philosophers and scientists) and Romantics, chiefly represented by practitioners of the humanities, to include some philosophers, who might be called the reciprocal radicals opposing the radical rationalists. In the details of the debate, the Romantic (as expressed by Keats and Lawrence) contends that the rationalist approach to the world or reality is not the most adequate way to understand that world or ourselves, preferring something rather like the "beautiful" referenced by Keats. The point of the Romantics is not to be a mindless anti-intellectual (with some exceptions) but to claim that reason and rationality are too narrow or even blinded in their focus by attenuated logical method. If this charge is true, the rational philosopher's picture of the world may be distorted because of the constraining tools and methodologies the philosopher employs.

The student reading these pages, therefore, should by now realize that with this kind of critique of philosophy, he is in the company of significant historical figures and movements echoing some of his own puzzlement or opposition over the way the philosopher works. Grasping this fact, he may now think his resistance to philosophy amply justified. Indeed, part of understanding and evaluating philosophy is acquainting oneself with various methods among philosophers, but likewise the swirl of arguments lodged against and among various philosophical methods or schools. All philosophers are not alike. This means that students may have different reactions to philosophy, based on the philosopher in their classroom. For example, student expectation for philosophy can be blunted or is gravely damaged by the student questioner being told his questions about life are not questions for philosophy. Any hopefulness for philosophy may then not only be diminished but destroyed for such a student. In enduring such constraints, the culture of doing philosophy in some classrooms may produce an understandable shock to students left reeling from the rigors of a philosophical method that makes every question fit the pet program of the philosopher. Some philosophers in such a classroom may be insistent upon a rationalistic methodology impugning everything except itself. Thus, such philosophers may be prone to force content to submit itself under concepts that may look rather contorted compared to the same objects in the "real" world. Moreover, for a student reeling under these procedures for detecting truth, he may most wonder when the method will show its application for and toward life. At other times, it may seem to the student that it is the immobile skeleton of the object or belief that an instructor looks at in the philosophy classroom. However, the beginning philosophy student has probably raised his philosophical questions as a being of flesh so to speak, and when in the classroom he is confronted with the skeletal question, he is confounded or resists such a method as too "abstract."

Furthermore, other philosophy teachers may substantially weaken or even sever the connection with philosophy that the questioning student may presume philosophy should have with life. This may be because the teacher is more like a technician who has perhaps resisted the philosophical questions posed by life. In short, this philosophy teacher may have separated questions about real life from what he terms real philosophy and foregone any pursuit of wisdom for pursuit of methodology.

The Existentialist school of philosophy in the mid-twentieth century was something of a revolt by a sector of philosophers who perceived that philosophy of their day was sunk in an analysis of problems that for the most part had little to do with the lives of real people. These renegade philosophers were also notable as novelists and playwrights and poets and essayists because for them, academic philosophy had simply grown too academic and, too far from real life or worse, had nothing to do with real life. They therefore lurched toward the literary and away from the mathematical and scientific that had become an earmark of certain schools of philosophy within the Western world.

Emphasis upon correct methods and correct methodology, of course, has been more a trait of some schools of philosophy than others. It was perhaps most recently exemplified in the logical positivists of the 1920s and 1930s who attempted in effect to modify the image of the philosophical enterprise for the scientific one. They regarded as "meaningless" many of the traditional questions of philosophy. From this insistence grew the famous discussion over verification that preoccupied thinkers in this tradition for some time. In the heyday of this philosophy of positivism, any philosophy that veered away from the logical and presumed scientific techniques of positivist philosophy was given the choice of calling itself "poetry" or "nonsense." The positivist's judgment upon any discourse as "poetry" was for them an assumption of the difference and the distance between scientific philosophy (their own) and other forms of discourse.

Reminiscent of the Existentialist revolt of a half century earlier, postmodern thought has attempted some relief from the strain of rationalism in much of modern philosophy. With postmodernism, there is an attempt to subjugate and seemingly punish an inherited rationalist tradition. However, what we might call the two approaches of razors or roses (reason and Romanticism, respectively) might complement or supplement each other, rather than each disowning the other.

The Romantic, existentialist or postmodernist charge that philosophy leans too heavily on the rational end of things, elicits various responses from traditional philosophers, though most in the end will uphold some commitment to reason as more beneficial to life with its presence rather than its absence. Even if it is conceded that reason is to be tempered by other considerations, such as those expressed by Keats and Lawrence, few philosophers will go down the route of wholesale abandoning or repudiating the use of reason. Therefore, one large issue of contemporary philosophy is to critically evaluate reason as the traditional tool of the philosopher in the way that the reason of philosophy has previously evaluated other things. Now the "other" is striking back, or so the postmodernist might contend. This is one reason that power is so often a subject of postmodern philosophers.

The argument for reason, however, would contend that without the defense and bulwark of reason, we are simply and totally defenseless. That is, and extending this possibility down the road of actually disowning reason entirely, it would seem rather a closed case that if my reason can retain no defensible confidence in itself, then I can make no objection to anything my reason tells me is awry or objectionable or simply dead wrong. That is, once I have given up on any and all confidence in the use of my reason, then I have the predicament of being absolutely vulnerable for anything. That is, I might as well believe anything, for I would lack the competence to make any judgments at all. For in taking this route, I have conceded the inability of reason to make any judgments. Of course, reason may not be the only horse to journey through life with but to put it out to pasture or into the grave would be to go too far. With reason, life may indeed be dangerous, but without it at all, I may be left with little defense, or for that matter, no defense.

Sometimes the Existentialists seemed, and certainly many postmodernists also seem, headed intently in such a dire direction, for with postmodernism, there is a loosening of commitment to rationality and science as the exclusive carriers or defenders of truth. This move was and is disdainful to traditional rationalists. Some thinkers, and paradoxically among them some repentant philosophers, are seen as undermining the traditional goal of thought and reflection in taking the postmodern route. In the conflict between the two, there is some resemblance of postmodernism to the Romantic resistance to the rationalism of the modern Enlightenment.

## 3.2 The Competition of Philosophy

Not infrequently academics from other disciplines and particularly the sciences judge philosophy a subject illicitly persisting when it should perish for its paltry contribution to knowledge. The comparison is usually made to the vast fund of knowledge contributed by the various sciences. From this perspective, while philosophy may have raised interesting questions or even important issues in the past, it nevertheless has the character of an idle spectator hanging on persistently in an adult world. Therefore, the student hostile to philosophy may now find another—but a different kind of critic of philosophy this time—making more unkind though different judgments about philosophy, and thus, another ally may be enlisted by this student in his resistance toward philosophy. To understand some of the particulars of this criticism and attitude toward philosophy, a bit more of the history of philosophy must be reviewed in terms of its relationship with other knowledge. In contrast to the Romantic aversion to the rationalism of philosophy, this perspective from largely scientific quarters will fault philosophy for not being rational enough. Thus, much of this kind of criticism of philosophy we might label as coming from "scientism." In its most severe form, this perspective would contend that philosophy is unneeded in the present day and age because we have science.

Whereas ancient philosophy displaced or at least weakened the mythological explanation of phenomenon, in time many of the speculations of philosophers will be assessed and sometimes fatally judged by the empirical method of science that gains footing in the early modern period of Western history. Moreover, while in the beginning, philosophers may be responsible for the plethora of questions issuing from the human mind hungry for knowledge, science brought order to the disorder of rampant speculation. Thus, we might compliment philosophy as the mother of the sciences because it produced children, but the children are raised by a parenting science. That is, once the empirical method of science becomes a veritable vessel for nailing down answers and separating truth from falsity, then the philosopher's speculative answers to questions must live with the verdicts of empirical validation and falsification. Philosophy, even as the mother of the sciences, appears empty-handed afterward, because her offspring are no longer her own—though the genealogy and biography of the children are evidenced in prior philosophical questions raised and speculations offered. Astronomy begins as a matter of philosophical speculation, but chunks of this subject matter are slowly wrested from philosophy by the empirical scientific possibilities of adjudication.

With philosophy as a precipitator of the sciences, Aristotle's speculations about the nature of the heavenly bodies was just that—philosophical speculation that only later science could confirm or show as false on many points. In other words, as Aristotle wrote, philosophy arises in wonder. Wonder provokes questions, and philosophy captures the first human attempt to provide some answers to those questions. Today, however, anyone wanting to know the nature of the heavenly bodies consults an astronomer, not a philosopher.

The obvious question arising from this history is does philosophy survive this siphoning off of much of its subject matter, or, with graver words, does it survive at all in the advance of scientific knowledge? That is, philosophy may be conceded to be the mother of the sciences and an initial pioneer of knowledge, but that role may suggest a finite life, for philosophy may have made the original claim to a piece of land whose deed is now owned by someone else. Is its only remaining residence that of a forgotten graveyard, where past glories now lie silent and unappreciated in the grave? Can philosophy redefine or reconfigure itself after science or should it continue to make its way alongside it?

Ignoring for the most part the porousness of any absolute border or wall dividing science from philosophy, philosophers have nevertheless been aware of the paucity and meagerness of their musings when comparing philosophy with the sciences. Of course, such a contrast is most evident and accentuated in the modern age, where science has such prestige. In light of the difference, consider, for example, what the psychologist B.F. Skinner (1904–1990) in his book *Beyond Freedom and*

*Dignity* wrote about the archaic but persistent presence of philosophy as a veritable admission of temporal defeat in the march of knowledge.

> Twenty-five hundred years ago it might have been said that man understood himself as well as any other part of his world. Today he is the thing he understands least. Physics and biology have come a long way, but there has been no comparable development of anything like a science of human behavior. Greek physics and biology are now of historical interest only (no modern physicist or biologist would turn to Aristotle for help), but the dialogues of Plato are still assigned to students and cited as if they threw light on human behavior. Aristotle could not have understood a page of modern physics or biology, but Socrates and his friends would have little trouble in following most current discussions of human affairs.

However one may deride this criticism as issuing from a triumphalism predicted for the science of the modern age, it is nonetheless the case that philosophers, though they are supposed to have some of the most respectable minds one can imagine, have nevertheless seemed extraordinarily slow in accumulation by any measurement of knowledge. Leaps of knowledge seem not to be a trademark of philosophy, however intelligent the philosophers.

One might respond, however, by simply contending that while science got the easy questions, philosophy got the hard ones, and furthermore, philosophy hung onto those questions when other thinkers—some philosophers among them—abandoned them. Paradoxically and pitiably, one might also say that philosophy retains the most interesting questions of humans that no other discipline will have. However, we can also make the point that while presumably Skinner would have all fields of knowledge made amenable to scientific methodology—whether in fact or not they are capable of being dealt with in such a manner—a thinker like Socrates made the turn from the cosmos to the human with his philosophy for a reason. For Socrates, the business of philosophy is the human world and all that is part of that world, rather than philosophy attempting to give an account of the far reaches of the cosmos.

Socrates, but more so his notable pupil Plato, did produce a metaphysic to fill out their philosophical anthropology, but it is one that resonates with and attempts to provide direction to the human world in a way that enunciating the four primary elements of earth, fire, wind, and water, for example, have provided little to aid the philosophical project on the human. In other words, in this Socratic tradition of philosophy, philosophy is conceived humanistically, even as it reaches to the world of the transcendent. Philosophy is about life, and not the life of the stars.

However, Skinner and others like him will have none of this staked out territory reserved for philosophy, simply because philosophy lacks the tools of science so as to ever decide answers to the questions posed. Because such a view favors success and scientific method over bumbling and failing philosophers, some philosophers on occasion have conceded something of the notable differences in favor of science, lecturing, or, more mercifully perhaps, attempting a revisioning of philosophy to be more like the successful sciences. In its severest modern form, moreover, an attempt to retool philosophy can become so radical that all that remains of philosophy in such a venture is the residual of, but hardly the reality of philosophy as historically understood. Many of the essential questions of philosophy are simply lampooned as unanswerable. This, of course, means unanswerable by science. It is no accident that philosophers taking this tact were no more hospitable toward theology answering such questions than they were philosophy. Philosophy proved to be something of an embarrassment to such thinkers, as had theology earlier to some philosophers stirred to assert the autonomy of philosophy against theology. Now, however, philosophy was fighting for its life, as science was demanding ownership of the philosopher's questions. Those questions that could not make the journey were largely ignored or mocked.

In our day, however, philosophy may be observed in a role as an attendant to science and thus is more often a second-order discipline in any association with science. That is, as a philosopher of science, for example, one will theorize about the meaning and nature of a theory and the nature of the relationship between the individual fact or the sum total of the facts and the theories that subsume those facts in science.

Such an example can help one see that philosophy is a kind of theorizing and that philosophy can indeed work in places where we know a little or a lot. It is, therefore, not only composed of people such as the pre-Socratics raising the first questions conjured up by the human mind. In time, moreover, the philosopher will not seek to reduplicate the work of the scientist, which would be a redundancy, but to ask questions that in some form are outside the current realm of scientific methodologies and procedures.

If philosophy is humankind's most strenuous attempt to arrive at real knowledge, and science grows out of and with philosophy, we need to ask if this is the extent of our human knowledge. That is, do we have any other sources of knowledge? Some would say yes, but others, no. For those who say yes, that other source might be in God through Divine revelation, articulated in the discipline referred to as theology, which literally means the science of God. If this is the case, then, we might broadly characterize the relationship between these various disciplines and their origins in the following manner.

### God > Divine Revelation > Theology Philosophy Science < Philosophy < Humans

With such a configuration, we can easily imagine the factional conflicts ensuing from the amalgamation of these various disciplines collectively attempting to arrive at a justification for themselves pursuant to a goal called truth. Of course, as suggested in this chapter, there will in all probability be hostility between and among these disciplines. So, for example, theology might deny legitimacy to philosophy, while philosophy may impugn or even ignore the claims of theology. We have already seen Skinner deny any legitimacy to philosophy from the perspective of science.

In general, it seems fair to say that all these various disciplines have truth as a goal but that their disagreements come about over what vehicles are deemed appropriate and reliable in that venture. In this context, it might be helpful to mention another human activity as part of the endeavor for knowledge and truth, namely art. Most artists today might shy away from depicting art as a pursuit of truth and prefer to think of the relationship between the two as art explicating and expressing truth. A postmodern artist would likely quibble even with this description because of the offending last word. That debate aside, however, we might envision these four human fields and practices, each with distinctive vehicles, judged as adequate by themselves, in terms of the goal of knowledge and truth. Disagreements and competing contentions that theirs is the better or more reliable—or maybe the only route to such a goal are sure to ensue. Thus, for example, we might say the distinctive trait of the sciences is facticity, philosophy that of reason, art that of inspiration, and religion that of revelation. Some thought would suggest that if we had to pair these four, we would probably put science and philosophy together, and art and religion together. One must be careful, however, not to think that the distinctive trait of each discipline in no way belongs to any other discipline. Hence, part of the disagreement and the discussion is apt to be over what each shares with some or all of the others, rather than with what each exclusively owns.

If philosophy is characterized by the use of reason and a certain rationalism, art might be thought to be a subject matter that philosophers would tend to neglect, and in great part, that suspicion is true. Moreover, some philosophers, perhaps most famously Plato, have been severe critics of art and artists. As we saw, however, in the allusions to John Keats and D.H. Lawrence previously, artists are not particularly agreeable to the judgment of philosophers. As implied by both Keats and Lawrence, the human is not just a brain with a conceptualizing intellect, for Keats portrays attention to sensation as missing from the philosopher's keen attention to intellect and thought, while Lawrence cites the philosopher's neglect of body as a reason to be suspicious of people who forget their material being. The animosity that sometimes breaks out between philosophy and art, moreover, is in part due to the association of emotion and imagination with art, and intellect and cognition with philosophy. Again, however, the similarities might be greater than the differences posited.

One might contend, moreover, that the work of the philosopher is somewhat analogous to the artist, in terms of the mode of working and how each is seen by the world. Furthermore, we might even envision and speak of an esthetic of philosophy and philosophers. Perhaps toward that end, we might even soften or make desirable the image of philosophy and philosophers as oddities—where we started this little book. To that hopeful end, we will turn in our last chapter.

**Name:** _____        **Date:** _____

1. What are the hesitations of the Romantic toward
   the philosopher and are such hesitations justified as
   criticisms of the philosopher?

2. What are the hesitations of many scientists in the modern world with the continuation of philosophy in the modern world and are such hesitations concerning philosophy justified?

# Chapter 4

# The Definition of Philosophy and Philosophers

## 4.1 The Challenges of Philosophy

Philosophy appears difficult to define, for philosophy has no subject matter for which philosophy claims sole ownership. This feature of philosophy contributes to the appearance of a certain emptiness surrounding the subject, though this trait of philosophy is also one of its strengths and serves to show that philosophy can raise questions about everything. Thus, what distinguishes philosophy is not precisely its subject matter, but the kind of questions it may fashion about anything. Philosophy inculcates the practice of asking why, and for that we have accumulating knowledge prodded by incessant questions that only sleep and stop when we do.

The upside of the seeming emptiness of the subject, again, is that the discipline of philosophy can go virtually anywhere, that is, to any subject. Thus, whereas botany is defined by the study of plants, zoology the study of animals, architecture the study of building forms, physics the study of matter and energy, entomology the study of insects, philosophy by contrast is defined more by method than by content. This is to say that because philosophy can focus its attention upon nearly any subject, it is the perspective and procedures and methods of philosophy that reveal more about it than subject matter. It is the way philosophy approaches a subject that provides a clue to what philosophy is. Paying close attention to this particular point about a discipline that owns no subject matter per se explains much about philosophy. A philosopher can take an interest in sports, laughter, artificial intelligence, or a myriad of other subjects that happen to interest him. There are, of course, better-known and well-known subjects philosophers work at such as metaphysics, epistemology, and ethics, but philosophy as a discipline is open to look at and work on almost anything. Philosophy may on occasion be thought of as stifling with its seemingly endless questions and points of view and perennial arguments, but it is also hugely self-guided with the philosopher free to choose where he works.

All the same, philosophy is a subject that presents some out-of-the-ordinary problems for students, beginning with the usual meandering attempt to define the difficult-to-define *"philosophy."* The teacher of philosophy may start his introduction to the subject by defining the word philosophy by its etymology—the love of wisdom—but such a definition by itself is of little help to students not already acquainted with the subject. This definition might understandably convey to beginning students that their grandparents, perhaps, as dispensers of wisdom, must have been or are philosophers.

This necessitates that we make a distinction among those different persons we would count as philosophers. We could start by claiming that to some degree, all people qualify as philosophers. This is simply because "ordinary" people consider many questions during a lifetime and many of them are correctly accounted philosophical questions. So, for example, the question that most people think of as the premiere philosophical question—the meaning of life—is surely a question approached or mulled over or thought about a little or extensively by quite a few people, though they would not be identified in the newspaper or in history books as philosophers. Thus, we can look upon such persons, who are most if not nearly all of us, as lay philosophers of a sort. This is why, as indicated in Chapter 3, philosophy in the classroom should extend and not curb the natural appetites of curiosity and wonder and the sense of puzzlement that accompanies living. This is why, too, philosophy should not be presented as offering something, but nothing having nothing to do with life, for to do so drives away the large pool of philosophers in training we have in classrooms for a season. That is, we want to convey to "ordinary" people that philosophy can aid us in living more meaningful lives even if we never step into another classroom of philosophy or undergo more exposure to the academic subject of philosophy.

Under the academic subject identified as philosophy, by contrast, we do not ordinarily read lay philosophers on the subject of philosophy. Rather, we tend to study those people making the subject of philosophy and the questions of philosophy their life's work, just as we might read a medical doctor or a medical researcher on a medical subject or a forester on something on forestry. The lay philosopher does other things during the day; the academic philosopher's days and perhaps some sleepless nights too, are devoted to the subject. Furthermore, our grandparents, and probably most of us, have not written down our philosophical musings in the interest of sorting things out in any definitive or systematic manner. There is little mystery to the noticeable distinction between the lay and the professional philosopher, for professional philosophers are often enlightening but also difficult to read. The lay philosopher is probably easier to read, but often not as enlightening.

As a subject of focus, this topic shows up in two different but related worlds. There is a "wide" sense of philosophy, in which everyone is a philosopher by the mere fact of being a curious and inquisitive human being, who at one time or another has thought about some of the great philosophical questions, provoked by curiosity, anxiety, pain, observation, happiness, unhappiness, or another particular experience. Virtually all people have philosophical interests of a sort, but at the same time, some people formally take up the subject matter by devoting their careers to it. This is the "narrow" sense in which philosophy is an academic study or discipline in the Academy and a subject matter to which some people devote their lives or careers.

To yet again define our subject by circling it, we could indicate that philosophy might best be understood as asking some of the most interesting questions imaginable. This is partly because its questions speak to the human condition, and so unlike what we said thus far, philosophy does seem to own some questions—Skinner providing an example of a negative proof of that. Moreover, philosophy has traditionally been thought of as devoted to questions that are lacking answers, or at least generally agreed-upon answers. This is largely because philosophy is the first human practice to raise a question and the last one to concede an answer. Philosophy works on the rough frontier in the beginning, but also, later, in town or teeming civilization, it continues by aiding in keeping things in order or revamping some existing structures. This means that philosophy can be something of a pioneer in the birthing of knowledge, but also a doubter or fixer regarding some huge and established edifices of learning.

In yet another way of defining or describing philosophy, we might say philosophy expresses our most primordial but also our most finessed attempt at knowledge. This means that our inquisitiveness prompts us—indeed, tempts us, no, rather forces us to inquiry about what we do not know, and thus philosophy represents a first fledgling attempt to arrive at knowledge where we once had ignorance. This venture is what often gives philosophy its speculative and theorizing nature. It is trying to map the landscape when little of the terrain is known. This is why philosophy belongs at the groundbreaking ceremony for virtually every project that has knowledge and understanding as its intent—and especially when that work involves where to start or even how to begin.

So the best description of philosophy might be recognizing it is an enterprise noticeably defined by its method, and its method is one of constant and relentless questioning and reasoning until a prospective solution or desired satisfaction seems plausible or possible. Solutions or answers, however, are not the prominent feature of philosophy, but its questions. Because of this the charge of no discernible progress of knowledge in philosophy is commonplace, but this criticism ignores the fact that philosophy is committed to working where knowledge is not present and ignorance has not been removed. This also often means that philosophy will move on after something is decided or a question answered. In this manner, philosophy generally gives way to science, which now tells us about the structure of the heavens, rather than the philosopher Aristotle who was read as the authority on such a question for almost two millennia after his death. The paucity of any dazzling amassing of knowledge from philosophy is not an embarrassment to philosophy, for philosophy changes directions when knowledge establishes itself. In this manner, philosophy, we might say, returns to the dark where there are other puzzles to solve. However, when there are some signs and directions in place, philosophy may have to work around these signposts, even as it may dispute some of them.

There are some questions of philosophy that do seem to a significant degree owned by philosophy. One can explain this fact by reference to some of the traditional questions associated with philosophy: the meaning of life, the surety of human knowledge, and the nature of reality. To some degree those questions prompted the first philosophers onto the stage of history, and the questions have generally stayed with the philosopher ever since, with some qualifications. For example, the nature of the cosmos or heavens has not remained with philosophers, for that study became astronomy and was subsumed under a branch of science. This was because the expertise and tools of science and scientists developed to a degree enabling some definitive verdicts on the speculative guesses of the philosopher and the scientist. If the scientist in time displaced the philosopher, the scientist at the same time valued and exercised the ability to speculate about possible hypotheses. It was Einstein who said that a good imagination was the first prerequisite for a good scientist. With enough scrutiny, the distinction between science and philosophy and even some of the human tools and abilities used by each can blur some of the distinctions between them.

In a different trajectory, philosophy has a hand in supplanting prior and existing knowledge, for it competes with other traditions within culture for assuming the mantle of knowledge. In this way, philosophy can be conceived as a kind of latecomer in human history. By this we mean—to take the case of the ancient Greeks as an example—Greek science and Greek philosophy came after Greek mythology. As the new kid on the block, so to speak, it must understandably compete and maybe dislodge competitors or opponents and show its mettle in so doing. However, the point here is that philosophy in part has a prickly aspect to its demeanor because it comes into a cultural world that is already fashioned in some form and with some reputable people and practices and institutions. Philosophy therefore has to position itself in the context of where it finds itself, within a world already up and running and making pronouncements and laws and such, even before philosophy may have raised its inquisitive head.

Just as philosophy has not only a myriad of subjects it can take up to philosophize about, it can also interject itself into the pursuit of knowledge at a number of places. It can work in the dark as we indicated, where scarcely anything at all is known, and thus philosophy can pioneer knowledge in places where there was virtually none to be found previously, or it can also compete with other practitioners and seekers of knowledge to supplant or correct some existing knowledge. It can in addition also descend upon some of the most elaborate and sophisticated knowledge to produce questions protruding from an admittedly impressive bastion of knowledge that might have presumed to render unnecessary any future questions being asked—until the philosopher turns up or returns.

All this is to say that as the human quest for knowledge has added to the fund of knowledge, philosophy has experienced no appreciable insignificance. In a culture where science reigns supreme, it can be often difficult to discern this presence of philosophy. Although philosophy may be culturally marginalized in a highly technical culture or frowned upon by a staid or primitive culture, the fact remains that philosophy seems wedded to the human person and human culture in a way that seems irresistible to some people and probably will be forever.

However, a student still trying to determine what accounts for the staying power of philosophy may think that the philosopher simply loves the question more than a final answer and is therefore committed to maintain the question at the cost of excluding the answer. However much we may associate the philosopher with the questions rather than the answer, few philosophers are committed to an enterprise in which they walk in a circle for the sake of only walking. Only in the so-called postmodern age of philosophy are there philosophers showing so little dedication or respect for truth as to mock the very notion.

The realization that traditional philosophy, however, is in business for the "long haul" forces us closer to the point of the question about the business of philosophy. That is, is philosophy dedicated to questions for the sake of the questions, and are answers realistically simply too much to hope for in light of the very long ages in which most questions of philosophy have been discussed? There are two competing justifications of philosophy on this question among various philosophers, though individuals can operate with some of both, sometimes dependent on the question. On the one hand, philosophy is undertaken and pursued in hope of an answer, in which case the questions of philosophy are perceived as legitimate given the intent of asking the questions: answers. This conception in no way intimates that answers are necessarily around the corner, but it does maintain the hope for answers that justifies the extraordinary time spent on the questions. This conception might be characterized as the classical position and seems the implicit hope of most lay philosophers.

However, there is another conception of philosophy famously stated by Gotthold Lessing (1729–1781) the modern German thinker who wrote:

> The worth of a man does not consist in the truth he possesses, or thinks he possesses, but in the pains he has taken to attain that truth. For his powers are extended not through possession but through the search for truth. In this alone his ever-growing perfection consists. Possession makes him lazy, indolent, and proud. If God held all truth in his right hand and in his left the everlasting striving after truth, so that I should always and everlastingly be mistaken and said to me, Choose, with humility I would pick on the left hand and say, Father grant me that; absolute truth is for thee alone.

Lessing's point is that one can prize the search along with the seizure, for the search inculcates a habit of humility and humbleness sufficient to make suspicious any claim to final truth. This conception of philosophy is therefore humanistic in intent, but at the same time scientific in its tentativeness and tends to be embraced by many modern philosophers.

## 4.2 The Rewards of Philosophy

We might venture the probably offending observation to some readers—though probably not to the reader who has read this far—that truth be told, philosophy is not for everybody. This is not because philosophy forbids us to enter but because many persons forbid significant questions to enter their world. That is, philosophy can be bothersome because it provokes us to stop and consider, or reconsider. The realization that questions of philosophy resist easy and quick answers may be disappointing to many students, but what prods others to engage in philosophy may just as well be the taunting question hiding its answer. That is, what can draw a student to philosophy may be the nature of questions seeming to defy answers most, for many such questions have been attractive to philosophers precisely because they have been perennial questions most resistant to yielding answers. The philosopher, moreover, who is prepared to accept this challenge, will not identify failure with the inability to give an answer to the questions in an afternoon. The requirement for patience needed for the long haul is not a universal human trait by any means, but most philosophers are reconciled to the fact that it is the nature of the questions they ponder that fast and effortless solutions are practically impossible. Consequently, patience is a needed prerequisite for doing philosophy.

However, there is a further point to be made here that puts the personality of the philosopher under some strain for others, and one might call it the solitude of the philosopher. This occurs with Socrates when the friends of Socrates propose that if he will parade his family in front of his accusers, his accusers might have some leniency for the accused. Socrates, however, will not budge and insists that the fact that he has a family has no relevance to his guilt or innocence of the charges against him. One might ask what his spouse thought of this kind of objection on the part of her husband. In other words, surely the demise and death of Socrates might have future benefits for the rights and respect accorded reason. Meanwhile, however, she gives up a husband who seems only too willing to pay the price of his life while she inherits the difficulties associated with losing a husband and bread-winner.

Other notable philosophers have been somewhat reclusive and regimented such as the German Immanuel Kant (1724–1804). Kant was extraordinarily punctual; the story is told that housemaids set their watch by the perfect time with which he made his walk in Konigsberg. He was not well traveled, but quite interestingly, he particularly enjoyed the company of people who had traveled extensively. He is said to have often surprised these visitors with his intimate knowledge of geography, a knowledge acquired, however, from reading and his guests and visitors, not his own travels. Kant, we might say, was a home body. All kinds of people can be a philosopher.

Katharine Tait, the daughter of Bertrand Russell, noted the solitude of her famous father in her fascinating book, *My Father Bertrand Russell*:

> He never gave his whole heart to anyone, though he tried. 'My most profound feelings have remained always solitary and have found in human things no companionship,' he wrote. 'The sea, the stars, the night wind in waste places, mean more to me than even the human beings I love best, and I am conscious that human affection is to me at bottom an attempt to escape the vain search for God.'
>
> We who loved him were secondary to the sea and stars and the absent God; we were not loved for ourselves, but as bridges out of loneliness. We were part of a charade of togetherness acted by a fundamentally solitary person. He played at being a father in the same way, and he acted the part to perfection, but his heart was elsewhere and his combination of inner detachment and outer affection caused me much muddle suffering.

This oddity or "estrangement" from others, we might remember, was a trait that was mocked by thinkers such as Erasmus. Nevertheless, despite the propensity of philosophers for questions, philosophers are not necessarily ones to seek out trouble; indeed, many prefer to avoid it. Even Russell himself makes an admission like this in his *Autobiography*, where Russell indicates that he always desired peace with all men. But more telling about philosophers is that they attempt to engage their peers and their public with their pens and not their swords. In doing so, the philosopher concedes that there is something outside themselves to which they make appeal. This would be argument of a certain kind.

The philosopher as a philosopher will be insistent to see the evidence in any argument or point of view and will caution that without any supporting premises, the point of an argument will be fruitlessly debated. This is because there can be no real debate when conclusions are only met with counter conclusions and both lack any evidence. So the philosopher does not just argue but fashions arguments that are in principle able to be decided by something more than shouting. This then means that to see the philosopher as a radical does not mean to necessarily see him as breathing fire or as the loudest or most obnoxious orator. The philosopher may be the person on the sideline who is scarcely heard over all the harangue. It is therefore, and again, very possible to miss the influence of the philosopher, because he may not even have the stage, but instead be in the audience. Because the philosopher may have the reputation of busting things up, we can simply miss the fact that the philosopher may also be putting things back together, as Descartes tried to vindicate knowledge in the face of the denial by the skeptics of his day. So the philosopher is scarcely a word slinger who talks first and asks questions later.

In trying to get to the truth of his subject or object or problem, the philosopher refuses the conventional weapons of human conflict because he would probably be inept if he tried to mount his defense with them, reminiscent of what Erasmus said about the practical inabilities of philosophers in Chapter 1. He therefore tries to force any adversary to fight on neutral terrain, where the weapons of conflict are argument and reason. Here the truth or real knowledge might be conceivable or ascertained, but there is another and much more significant reason for the philosopher refusing to abide by the often roguish disarray rife in some disagreements. The philosopher refuses to concede that "might makes right." For the philosopher, might does not define what is right; thought, reason, and argument should. In this way, the potential or in fact maybe the actual material victory of the competitor may be rendered hollow or perhaps even humiliating to a victor, such as the verdict of the Athenian jury might have appeared compared to the condemned but unphased Socrates. The apparent victor may have only proved his superior might. The question of whether he is right has still to be considered. Seen in this light, the philosopher may be seen as the voice of reason or as the prophet for peace, but if this is so, then the philosopher paradoxically is not always an upsetter of the peace. Instead, he can aid in keeping the peace or even have a role in establishing it.

Of course, as is the case in a lot of conflict, oftentimes conflict is a war of personalities. But just as the philosopher refuses to settle a question of right or truth by a material showdown, the philosopher does not want to relegate such goals as right and truth to the mercy of powerful personalities. Moreover, a war of words sometimes betokens a war of personalities, because the combatants have nothing greater than their individual personalities with which to settle their conflict. We therefore have need of rule by law or argument or reason or moral persuasion. There is therefore a "measure" outside the individual that governs the individual. The traditional philosopher makes appeal to this thing outside the individual, whether to argument or objectivity, but in the interest, ultimately, of truth. Seen in this light, the philosopher is not always a radical upsetter of the peace and indeed at times exhibits the near purity of a child desirous of knowing something unknown or making something right that was wrong.

The philosopher's quest to know, therefore, has a certain esthetic quality about it. That is, it is the sheer delight in knowing that often propels in people the desire to know. Aristotle, of course, represents this notion in his description of the justification of knowledge as knowledge gained for its own sake. This notion points to no explicit practical end or justification for knowledge beyond itself. However, part of what makes philosophy spurned and unpopular is that by questioning existing notions, customs, tradition, and so forth, philosophy in effect asks one to go back and reconsider many beliefs we have. Philosophy in a sense then asks one to start again. In this capacity, philosophy allows us or pushes us in some way to be a child again. The childlikeness of philosophy, however, can produce a feature opposite the innocence of a child.

That is, even though to a child everything is new, adults in time give an impression of permanence to things that philosophy may challenge as much as a child questioning adults about why they do or think things they think or do. This facet of philosophy, therefore, gives it a characteristic that is the opposite of childlikeness: its potentially radical and revolutionary character. In philosophy, no stone remains unturned. In philosophy, one can reopen what may have been deemed a closed matter.

Rene Descartes illustrates this paradoxical facet of philosophy. Descartes wanted to establish some solidity for knowledge under the threat of a revived skepticism, but to do so, Descartes went back to doubt everything, he says, that he had previously thought. In effect, Descartes is going to start again. In starting again, of course, he is going to subject his current beliefs to scrutiny, and he in fact is going to allow philosophy—or in his specific case doubt—to rattle his cage. Thus, the radical nature of the philosophical enterprise results. Descartes does philosophy upon himself, but with a figure like Socrates, who turns philosophical scrutiny upon other people's beliefs, the effect can be one of great personal unpopularity for the philosopher. Meanwhile, the philosopher may have a solace and peace or contentment denied by his accusers or detractors. Although philosophers, of course, will exhibit personal differences here, or as we said in our last chapter, all philosophers are not alike. Some can look like bulls in china shops because they have a keen desire to get to the bottom of things, to get it right. This represents their inquisitive bent. They will therefore often be as tenacious about eradicating error as they are about discovering truth. Although all philosophers are "critical thinkers" in the ordinary sense of that description, some philosophers tend more to the side of negative criticism, whereas others tend to the side of being constructive thinkers. The latter, however, do not assume an uncritical eye, but they are the great system builders among the mass of philosophers—Aristotle, St. Thomas Aquinas, Hegel.

In the cases of both Socrates and Descartes, their ultimate intent is to discover some real knowledge and, thus, to distance themselves from skepticism or the claim that all supposed knowledge is really only merely opinion. That is, they are wanting to "clean house" so to speak, but the purpose of philosophical house cleaning is to put the philosophical house into proper order rather than to leave it a pile of rubble. The philosopher is usually not one to abide by the warning to "leave well enough alone." It may be the case that the house being examined is so replete with wrong wiring, plumbing, and so forth that little will be allowed to remain after the inspection is over. The inspection, therefore, may require a leveling or shaking of the foundations, but nevertheless, with a view toward "getting it right."

In this portrayal of the life of philosophy, philosophy may seem to many to have few alluring enticements or visible rewards, and this is one reason and maybe the most important reason for its small numbers. The argument of a critic here provides something by way of understanding why most of us are followers, or to speak more philosophically, asleep. It simply seems less tiring to most people to carry out the motions of living without asking for what or why are we living. Paradoxically, in a world of nearly constant movement, the movement of the philosopher may be scarcely noticed and indeed may provoke the appearance of people without motion, but then we are apt to miss the contributions of many of the great minds of our culture and civilization. Indeed, the contribution of a Socrates lies in his realism, which is perhaps most highlighted in the way he conducts himself at the trial that resulted in his execution. In his defense, Socrates makes his accusers look like defendants rather than prosecutors. It is they who are put upon the hot seat, as Socrates recounts their mistakes in subjecting him to what they should be subjecting themselves.

The world revealed by philosophy seems without any power to lure anyone but the philosopher, so what does the philosopher find so attractive or inviting about philosophy? Aristotle said that all people by nature desire to know, but the philosopher, of course, has an exceptional desire to know. Seen in this light, the perceived arrogance or radicalness of the philosopher is a misconception; the philosopher is simply prodded by a relentless search to know, or, like Socrates, he may count himself wiser for being aware of his ignorance when he is in fact ignorant. The philosopher acknowledges a master that others may not only scorn, but even disdain. The philosopher's practice, therefore, despite the appearance of living in a study seeming to exist only on perpetual theories or speculations, is to take his stand in the search for truth. The mistaken perception of arrogance in the philosopher, therefore, is undercut when we see that the philosopher is in fact humbled by the truth.

Philosophy, as we have said earlier, is famous for questions but not for answers. The charge that philosophy is simply a childish wrangle ignores the fact that the questions of philosophy are not like those of mathematics or empirical science, against which oftentimes everything else gets compared. Although most philosophical questions have not received answers of unanimity, the fact of the matter is that most philosophers and most people coming to and working through philosophical questions do take positions. Thus, just because people cannot agree on answers to the questions raised by philosophy does not mean that no one ever takes a position on anything unless everyone else is in agreement.

The question to really ask about philosophy is why people would return again and again to what many deem an empty plate or to questions that seem so stingy with answers It is questions, after all, that first lure and provoke people to become philosophers. However, why would people go to a job in which they were very rarely compensated for work in the form of visible or material wages or payment? That is, why do people return again and again to something that appears to rarely produce finality? Lessing's answer can provide some response to this question. Eventually, we should see too that the perpetual return of people to philosophy and philosophical questions is indicative that something in philosophy is prized enough to merit the proverbial return. This phenomenon is little different from the people who are not permanently but only temporally deferred by being turned down for a date by someone with whom they desire to establish a relationship. With philosophy, the perception is that the questions are so singularly intriguing or important that one can scarcely leave them alone. They are simply a perpetual draw for what many of them are: the questions of significant importance and interest to many people some of the time and some of the people all the time. John Hermann Randall, Jr., reminded us that philosophy is truthfully the oldest profession of humans. If this is the case, then philosophy is hardly unnatural to humans, nor is it likely to ever disappear for as long as there are humans.

**Name:** _____          **Date:** _____

1. Can philosophy be of benefit for people who are not professional philosophers and how could it benefit such people?

2. What traits of a philosopher might make him a valuable citizen and what traits of a philosopher might make him a nuisance to society?

# References

Erasmus, Desiderus. *Praise of Folly*.

Keats, John. *Letter of November 22, 1817 to Benjamin Bailey*.

Lawrence, D. H. "Why the Novel Matters."

Lessing, Gotthold. *Nathan the Wise*.

Murdoch, Iris. "Literature and Philosophy."

Plutarch. *Lives*.

Randall, John H., Jr. *The Career of Philosophy*.

Russell, Bertrand. *The Autobiography of Bertrand Russell*.

Russell, Bertrand. *The Principles of Social Reconstruction*.

Skinner, B. F. *Beyond Freedom and Dignity*.

Tait, Katharine. *My Father Bertrand Russell*.

CPSIA information can be obtained
at www.ICGtesting.com
Printed in the USA
LVOW05s2311240118
563651LV00005B/21/P